IDEAS TO SAVE
YOUR LIFE

THE 15-MINUTE
PSYCHOLOGIST

G000026478

IDEAS TO SAVE
YOUR LIFE

THE 15-MINUTE
PSYCHOLOGIST

ARCTURUS

ARCTURUS

This edition published in 2014 by Arcturus Publishing Limited
26/27 Bickels Yard, 151–153 Bermondsey Street,
London SE1 3HA

Copyright © Arcturus Holdings Limited

All rights reserved. No part of this publication may be reproduced,
stored in a retrieval system, or transmitted, in any form or by any means,
electronic, mechanical, photocopying, recording or otherwise, without
prior written permission in accordance with the provisions of the
Copyright Act 1956 (as amended). Any person or persons who do any
unauthorised act in relation to this publication may be liable to criminal
prosecution and civil claims for damages.

ISBN: 978-1-78212-643-0
AD003874UK

Printed in China

CONTENTS

What is psychology anyway?

The human brain is the single most compelling object of study or contemplation. Whatever other interests you may have – art, politics, literature, sport, mechanics, astronomy, chess – originated with a human mind and you use your own mind to pursue them. How the mind works, in sickness and in health, is the realm of psychology.

To know how and why and what we think has fascinated humankind for millennia, but until recently we had little other than metaphor and stories to help us express our ideas about our own minds' workings.

Brain and mind, body and spirit

In the 17th century, the French philosopher and mathematician René Descartes suggested that the human body follows mechanical laws and so works rather like a machine. We can apply fluid dynamics to explain how the blood flows, for instance, and our bones and muscles work just like levers. But Descartes could not work out how the spirit that animates the body – what would later be called 'the ghost in the machine' – fits in.

'I think therefore I am,' he said (in a different philosophical enquiry). We would probably all agree that it is principally our minds that make us who we are. In theory, your physical body could be occupied by another brain (if we had the surgical skill to effect a brain transplant) and that body would then no longer act for 'you' but for the person whose brain was residing in it. We locate the 'I' that is our identity in our mind, and our mind is somehow in, or created by, our brain.

To explain the mind in the brain, people have turned to stories and religions. Is it a spirit or soul breathed into us by a god? Is it a portion of some vast world or universal soul, a little chip off a cosmic block of consciousness? Today, we are getting closer to understanding how the brain works and although we still can't quite locate or define the mind, we can explain a lot of how it works in terms of neurology.

Psychology, psychiatry and neurology

Psychology is the study of how the mind (psyche) works. Psychiatry applies some of that knowledge therapeutically to help people with disorders of the mind. And neurology is the study of the physical and chemical structure and functioning of the brain. In studying 'how the mind works', psychology involves neurology in some of its explanations.

Mind how you go

Most of us have fairly healthy minds. We might be subject to some of the more common types of mental illness from time to time, just as our bodies have physical ailments. You might sometimes have anxiety problems, or have suffered a period of depression, or have obsessive-compulsive disorder (OCD), just as you might have had appendicitis or suffer from eczema or asthma.

BEHIND THE MASK

To many people, mental illness is more frightening than physical illness. We can't see what's going on. There's no rash or twisted limb to look at, so we can't imagine what the problem is or how severe it is. Many people feel threatened by any type of mental illness, even though someone with (say) OCD or depression is no threat at all to anyone else. We can't catch it, like we can catch flu.

As we start to understand how imbalances in the chemistry or errors in the structure of the brain cause some types of psychological problems, perhaps people will be less worried. After all, producing too little dopamine in the brain (associated with depression and Alzheimer's disease, among other conditions) is not conceptually any different from producing too little insulin in the pancreas (which causes type 1 diabetes).

We are the lab rats

For many of us, the most personally relevant aspects of psychology are how our minds work in everyday ways. How we learn, how we interpret the world, how we interact with other people and what we are like. To find out about these aspects of the mind, psychologists

often perform experiments, either in the laboratory or in the 'field' (out in the world), or carry out studies – asking questions or examining statistics, for instance. Only by looking at the behaviour or development of a large number of people can psychologists work out what falls in the middle of the spectrum – what we casually call 'normal'. Some psychology studies focus solely on dysfunctional minds. This is not only because dysfunctional minds might need special treatment and therapy but also because they help to shed light on 'normal' minds.

Hard work

Psychological studies are plagued with problems. If people know their behaviour is being investigated they often change it. They might do this for various reasons: to please the experimenter, to seem like the kind of person they would like to be, to be perverse or, perhaps unconsciously, because the alien situation of the laboratory set-up makes them anxious. That means that many studies have had to be surreptitious, and that raises ethical problems. Some of the landmark experiments in psychology would not be allowed by an ethics committee today. Subjects did not give consent for what was actually going to happen to them but often for something else entirely. And some experiments risked causing genuine psychological harm to the people selected – encouraging them to act in ways they would later regret, for example. Later on we will look at some examples of psychology experiments that had potentially damaging effects on their subjects.

Like-minded?

It's hard to say how far the results of a study can be extended to the general population, particularly to those of different cultures. The subjects are often of a certain type – people who readily agree or volunteer to be involved in experiments – and therefore are not necessarily typical of the population at large. Subjects are sometimes chosen from an even more specific group of people – students in or near a psychology department who are short of cash and therefore willing to take part in an experiment for the money. How far can results gleaned from

Are we all of one mind? How much is the working of the mind common to all humans, and how much is due to the way we live or were brought up?

studying affluent twenty-one-year-old American college students, for example, be extended to explain the behaviour of elderly Afghani goat-keepers, workers in a Bangladeshi garment factory, Tibetan nuns, or Brazilian business tycoons?

New approaches

Typically, psychology looks at our emotional state and behaviour. In the past, psychologists could only come to conclusions about how our minds work by paying heed to what we say and do. The physical structure of the brain was the realm of neurologists. But today, psychologists can also see the mind in action by using various brain-scanning technologies to reveal what the brain is doing at certain times and when we feel certain moods. As a result, neurology and psychology are coming closer together, even undertaking some joint ventures. So that's where we will start – with what we can learn from a brain. But thereafter we will roam more freely around the mind, only touching biological bases occasionally.

Burning questions

There are two very big, over-arching questions in psychology that stray into the realms of philosophy, evolutionary biology and jurisprudence. One is: to what extent is the mind the product of nature (our biological inheritance), or the result of nurture (our

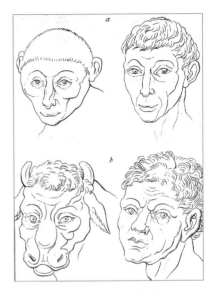

Physiognomic comparisons of a man and a monkey, and a man and a bull. The belief that an individual's inner character could be read in their outward appearance ('physiognomy') was popular during the 18th and 19th centuries; many writers of the period, such as Charles Dickens and Edgar Allan Poe, included physiognomic descriptions of characters in their work.

environment and upbringing)? The other is: to what extent can we be said to have free will and, consequently, be held responsible for our own actions? They overlap.

Some of the questions asked in this book deal with aspects of how much of our psychological make-up is hardwired and how much comes from the environment. Chapter 7 – *Is morality natural?* and Chapter 18 – *What do you see?* both touch on this. It seems that the basic structure of the brain gives us certain intrinsic gifts, such as an ability to learn language, and the ability to interpret what we see. These are abilities that each new human being does not need to learn from scratch. In other ways, we are the product of our environment.

Chapter 6 – *Does indulgence spoil a baby?* and Chapter 17 – *Can you spot a psychopath?* both touch on how upbringing can affect a person's mental health in later life.

If a lot of our behaviour is determined by brain chemistry or structure, or factors in early childhood over which we had no control, can we be held responsible for what we do? Many legal systems provide for people being less responsible if deemed mentally impaired, but this is quite a specific defence. The psychopath with the combination of brain structure and upbringing that makes it almost inevitable he will kill will still be locked up for murder. Recently, psychology has gone even further in undermining free will – the entire construct might be an illusion (see opposite). If people are doomed to follow certain paths, the issues of reward and punishment become quite complex.

Don't try this at home

The questions posed here are not, on the whole, related to mental disorders and the answers suggested are not intended as prescriptive. Please don't use this book to try to diagnose any mental problems in yourself or others. The book aims to take a peek at how the mind works, but it doesn't give definitive answers and it can't begin to cover all the approaches psychologists have taken. Oh, and please don't try reproducing any of the experiments described.

IS FREE WILL AN ILLUSION?

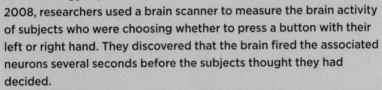

Studies of the brain in action have shown that when we think we are making a free choice, our brain has already started acting. In a neurology experiment conducted in 2008, researchers used a brain scanner to measure the brain activity of subjects who were choosing whether to press a button with their left or right hand. They discovered that the brain fired the associated neurons several seconds before the subjects thought they had decided.

Other experiments have found similar results. When brain scanners are used to monitor people who believe they are freely choosing to move parts of their body, the area of the brain that is preparing the movement is active for around a second before the person moves. The conscious intention to move and the movement itself happen at virtually the same time. It appears that – if we have free will at all – it isn't where we think it is. The feeling of deciding to move is our interpretation of something that has already happened in the brain. Some other part of the brain, of which we are unaware, has apparently decided on the movement and started it off. Then we get the feeling 'Ooh, I know, I'll move my hand,' by which time it's already happening. Spooky...

Perhaps those people who think they are controlled by aliens are right after all.

Chapter 1

What can we learn from a brain?

We can't watch the brain working like we can watch a heart pumping.

Psychology is the study of what goes on in the brain – thinking, learning, personality, dreams, desires, character formation, behaviour determination, and disorders of all of those. But unlike the study of what goes on in, say, the heart, there is no mechanical process to observe directly. So scientists have had to find some ingenious ways of monitoring our thought processes.

Viewing our thoughts

In the early days of psychology, the only way of looking at a brain directly was once its owner had died. All psychological study had to be by experimenting with, observing and questioning live brain-users. While all those techniques remain extremely useful today, we now have ways of viewing the living brain while it's doing its stuff. But viewing the brain raises as many questions as it answers. Knowing about the biology of the brain only takes us so far. We can see that it is

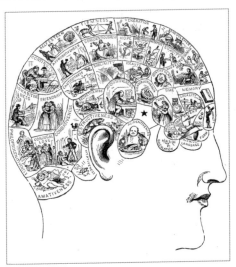

NEUROSCIENCE – THE BASICS

The brain is made up of lots of cells called neurons (nerve cells), which are responsible for producing neural activity. 'Lots' is around 86 billion. Neural activity includes receiving 'messages' from the receptors in the sensory organs located in different parts of the body and transmitting messages to activate the muscles, for example, in other parts of the body. Some actions are conscious, such as raising your arm; some are unconscious, such as increasing heart beat.

Different parts of the brain are responsible for different types of neural activity. Information from the eyes is transmitted to the visual cortex at the back of the brain and processed to produce the images we 'see' in the mind. Emotions, on the other hand, are processed in the amygdalae, two small structures located deep within the brain.

doing something, but we still can't see quite what it is doing, or how. We can see neurons firing as someone thinks, but can't see what they are thinking, or why they had that thought, or how they will remember (or forget) it.

Size matters

ANIMAL	NEURONS	ANIMAL	NEURONS
Fruit fly	100,000	Cockroach	1,000,000
Mouse	75,000,000	Cat	1,000,000,000
Baboon	14,000,000,000	Human	86,000,000,000

What goes where?

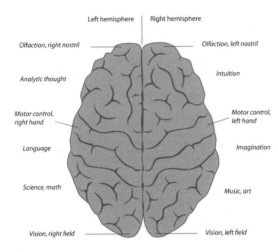

Lateralization of Brain Functions

Left hemisphere | Right hemisphere

Olfaction, right nostril

Analytic thought

Motor control, right hand

Language

Science, math

Vision, right field

Olfaction, left nostril

Intuition

Motor control, left hand

Imagination

Music, art

Vision, left field

For millennia, the only way to discover which parts of the brain were used for different functions was to observe people who had suffered head injury and note how that had affected their mental or physical abilities, mood or behaviour. The changes resulting from the head injury were a good indication that different parts of the brain were responsible for different functions (emotions, cognition, personality and so on). Post-mortem examination revealed brain damage that might be related to changes or impaired function noticed in the person when they were alive. To acquire meaningful insights into the workings of the brain, scientists needed lots of brains to examine and sophisticated scientific equipment to do it with. So the brain was pretty much a closed book until the 20th century. It's not a very open book even now.

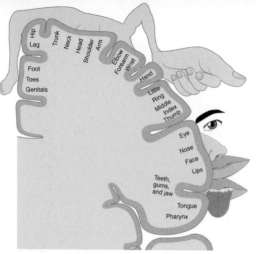

This diagram shows which areas of the brain correspond to the sensory input from different parts of the body. The relative size of the different body parts indicates how much of the brain is involved in processing the signals it receives, hence the hand is shown much larger than the foot.

The unfortunate Phineas Gage

The idea that specific parts of the brain might be responsible for different functions originated with the medical case of a railroad construction foreman called Phineas Gage. On 13 September 1848, Gage was seriously injured when a metal tamping iron – a long, pointed rod weighing six kilograms – was accidentally fired through his head. It entered through the cheek and left through the top of his head, taking fragments of his brain with it. He lost a bit more brain when he vomited, and 'about half a teacup full' of brain fell on the floor, according to the doctor who attended him. The main damage was caused to one of the frontal lobes of his brain.

Although his friends had a coffin ready and waiting for him, remarkably, Gage (right) lived. However, his personality changed considerably for a long period. Instead of the polite and friendly man he had been before, he became difficult and antisocial – though not the terrible character that legend suggests. His social ineptitude improved with time, and he ended his days working as a stagecoach driver in Chile. It's possible that the routine of his new life helped in his rehabilitation, as structured activity is found to be helpful in the treatment of many patients suffering damage to the frontal lobes.

In two minds

The brain comprises two halves, or hemispheres. Each hemisphere contains the same structures and there is communication between the two via a thick bundle of nerve fibres called the *corpus callosum*.

How the two hemispheres work together was explained by Roger W. Sperry, a neuropsychologist who treated patients with severe epilepsy by severing the *corpus callosum*. It sounds drastic, and it was, but it did cure their epilepsy. After he cut the connection between the two hemispheres, the right hand literally did not know what the left hand was doing.

At first the surgery appeared to have little impact on the patients – apart from relieving their epilepsy. But investigation of Sperry's split-brain patients soon revealed that there had been major changes. In the process, Sperry gained new insights into how the two halves of the brain normally work together.

> '[Each hemisphere is] indeed a conscious system in its own right, perceiving, thinking, remembering, reasoning, willing, and emoting, all at a characteristically human level, and... both the left and the right hemisphere may be conscious simultaneously in different, even in mutually conflicting, mental experiences that run along in parallel.'
> Roger Wolcott Sperry, 1974

Sperry found that if he presented a picture to the right visual field (processed by the left side of the brain), the patient could name the object in speech or writing, but if it was presented to the left visual field they could not.

They could, though, identify the object by pointing. From this, Sperry concluded that language is processed in the left side of the brain.

He found, too, that objects shown to the left side of the brain can only be recognized by that side. If he displayed different symbols in the right and left visual fields and then asked the person to draw what they saw, they only drew the symbol shown in the left visual field. If he then asked them what they had drawn (not seen), they described the symbol in the right visual field. Objects originally viewed in the left visual field were recognized if viewed again in the left, but not if then viewed in the right visual field.

Look inside

We no longer need to wait for people to die before we can look at their brains. There are various ways we can monitor or examine brain structure and activity:

- A computed tomography (CT) scan uses X-rays and a computer to produce three-dimensional images of the brain. It shows the normal structure and can highlight damage, tumours and other structural changes or abnormalities.
- An electroencephalogram (EEG) monitors the electrical impulses produced by brain activity. It can reveal the person's state of arousal (sleeping, waking and so on) and show how long it takes for a stimulus to trigger brain activity or reveal the areas where brain activity takes place when the subject performs an action or

LEFT BRAIN, RIGHT BRAIN?

In popular psychology, it's common to refer to 'left brain' and 'right brain' functions or personalities. If the left half of your brain is dominant (or so the story goes), you will be good at logical and analytical thought, and more objective than a right-brain thinker. If the right half of the brain is in charge, you'll be intuitive, creative, thoughtful and subjective. But it's nonsense. Almost all functions are carried out approximately equally by both halves of the brain. Where there are differences, there's variance between individuals as to which hemisphere does more of one thing or another.

$$(a - b)^3 =$$
$$= a^3 - 3a^2b +$$
$$+ 3ab^2 - b^3$$

The only area of significant difference is in language processing, as discovered by Sperry. The left hemisphere works at the syntax and meaning of language, while the right hemisphere is better at the emotional content and nuance of language. But that's it – not enough on which to build a 'left-brain = logical, right brain = creative' construct.

is exposed to a stimulus.

- A positron emission tomography (PET) scan reveals the real-time activity of the brain by showing where radioactively-tagged oxygen or glucose is being concentrated. This is because the harder the brain works the more oxygen and glucose it uses. It's useful for seeing which parts of the brain are used for specific tasks or functions.

- Magnetic resonance imaging (MRI) combines radio waves with a powerful magnetic field to detect different types of tissue and produce detailed anatomical images of the brain.

- Magnetoencephalography (MEG) picks up the tiny magnetic signals produced by neural activity. This is currently expensive and not widely used, but provides the most detailed real-time indication of brain function.

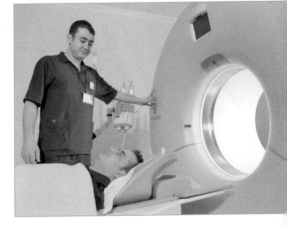

For the first time, brain scans show psychologists which parts of the brain are involved in different types of activity and behaviour. Comparing brain scans of psychopathic killers, for instance, shows that they all have similar brain abnormalities (see page 181).

Use it or lose it

If psychologists relied on studying damaged brains for their research, they would make slow progress. Luckily, healthy, functioning brains are just as useful.

In 2000, Eleanor Maguire at University College, London, used MRI scanning to compare the brains of London taxi drivers and a control group of men of similar age and profile. The taxi drivers spend up to four years memorizing routes through the 25,000 streets of London. This is known colloquially as the 'Knowledge'. Maguire's study showed that the posterior hippocampus of the taxi driver's brain is significantly larger than the hippocampus in members of the control group. This research not only indicated the importance of the hippocampus in navigation and spatial awareness but also that the brain (or at least the hippocampus) can adapt with regular use, building up like a muscle that strengthens with repeated exercise.

The longer the men had worked as taxi drivers, the more marked the difference. Maguire found in a follow-up study that in retired taxi drivers, who were no longer using the Knowledge and therefore not exercising the hippocampus so much, the size decreased to normal.

It's not possible to drive a taxi while being MRI scanned, but

DO YOU ONLY USE 10 PER CENT OF YOUR BRAIN?

Another popular psychology myth is that we only use 10 per cent of our brain. In fact we use all of our brain, though not all at the same time. It's quite likely that many of us don't use our brain to its full potential most of the time, but all areas of the brain have a function and you do use those functions during the course of a day or a week. You can always do more – when you learn new skills, your brain makes new connections between neurons to store knowledge and patterns of behaviour. But those connections are not there languishing empty, 'alone and palely loitering', and waiting to be filled.

Maguire was able to use a computer game that involved navigating around London to watch the taxi drivers' brains in action. She found the hippocampus was most active at the start of the task, when the driver had to think about and plan the route. Maguire's study was important not only in

showing which area of the brain is used for navigation, but also that it can adapt with increased stimuli – an ability that holds promise for people who have suffered brain damage and need rehabilitation.

Brains in jars

Long before we had modern imaging technologies, scientists supposed that if they were able to look at someone's brain they would be able to see physical differences between, for instance, very

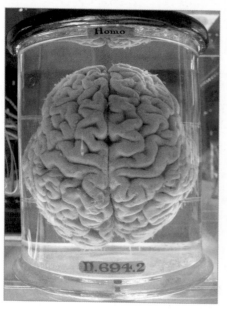

bright people and those of average intelligence, or violent criminals and law-abiding citizens. It didn't turn out to be that simple. For example, intelligent people don't have larger brains, as we might expect.

When Albert Einstein died in 1955, his brain was removed, examined, photographed and stored, disappearing for twenty years until it was rediscovered in 1978. The brain had been cut into 240

JUST THINK!

Brain-computer interface (BCI) devices pick up brainwaves and feed them directly into a computer. Using such devices, it has been possible to train macaque monkeys to move things using only their thoughts. In these experiments the monkeys' arms were restrained and a sensor the width of a hair was implanted in the brain to detect the signals that would normally go to the monkey's arm and so use them to control a robotic arm instead. This system is not yet regarded as safe for humans to use.

During the experiments a macaque monkey used the power of thought to move a robotic arm and feed itself marshmallows and fruit.

pieces for microscopic examination, which was a nuisance for later researchers. There was no size difference between Einstein's brain and 'normal' brains (that is, brains from those who were not Nobel prize-winning physicists). But there were some structural differences. Einstein's brain actually lacks a few of the features found in normal brains, and it's been suggested that this may have helped it to make neural connections more easily. The inferior parietal lobe of Einstein's brain was 15 per cent wider than others, and that area is used for mathematical thought, visualizing movement and spatial-visual cognition. There were also more connections between parts of his brain than is usual.

Looking at the brains of dead people also helps us to understand mental illness. The brains of people who had Alzheimer's disease show tissue loss and shrinkage.

With brain scans, we can see when people are thinking or dreaming, which part of the brain works on different activities and whether there are brain abnormalities or damage. But we can't yet see *what* people are thinking. Although seeing the thoughts of others would have serious implications for personal privacy, it could be very helpful for people who are paralyzed and unable to communicate.

Mind and body – who's boss?

Descartes struggled with the problem of how the mind and body could interact – of how the mental intention to lift a hand could be translated into the action itself. In fact, the brain seems to have far more sway over the body than that.

One of the strangest mental disorders is the rare Cotard's syndrome. Sufferers of this terrible condition believe that they are dead. Until the advent of brain scans, there was no explanation for how this could come about. But recent research has revealed some clues. It appears that in Cotard's syndrome the link between the senses and the limbic system and amygdalae, responsible for the emotions, is completely lacking. The consequence is that whatever the sufferer sees, hears, smells or touches arouses no emotional response at all. And the only way the person can rationalize their complete non-engagement with the world is by concluding that they are actually dead. Something that seems to be incontestable proof of madness (not a useful term at the best of times) actually has a rational basis, with the brain looking at the evidence produced by its damaged self and coming to a conclusion that seems to fit in all ways but one.

'Good Lord – my arm's off!'

According to neuroscientist Vilayanur S. Ramachandran, the extreme feelings of de-personalization and de-realization experienced by many people with depression and anxiety disorders may be due to a similar type of

'By God, sir, I've lost my leg!'
'By God, sir, so you have!'
Exchange between Lord Uxbridge and the Duke of Wellington at the Battle of Waterloo, 1815

mechanism, but on a smaller scale. A temporary disconnection might account for the well-documented phenomenon of people not feeling or being aware of traumatic injury at times of great stress. In an emergency, the amygdalae shut down and the anterior cingulate cortex, located deep in the brain, becomes hyperactive. This structure keeps you alert and so helps you make the right response to a given situation. This is the trick the brain is using in the case of soldiers in battle who don't feel it when a leg is blown off.

In sickness and in health

We have all heard of psychosomatic illness – physical ill-health for which there is no physical cause. There are many physical symptoms associated with stress, depression and extreme emotion, including headaches, vomiting, stomach ache and muscles pains. We are also familiar with the placebo effect of treatments that have no active pharmacological components but still make people feel better. It is well documented that if people believe they are receiving a potent or effective medicine, they will often get better even if they are only being given sugar pills. Many people suspect that at least some alternative therapies work through the placebo effect – when they work at all.

Perhaps even more surprising and compelling evidence of just how far the brain can control the body comes from the reverse of the placebo effect, called the 'nocebo effect'. This is when illness or even death is triggered by a harmless substance, just because the subject expects there to be a harmful effect. Around 25 per cent of people given a placebo in a drug trial will develop the side effects they were told to expect from the real drug.

... especially sickness

People who die after being cursed are a prime example of the nocebo effect in action. A voodoo practitioner, for example, who believes in the efficacy of a curse will often die when cursed himself, even though there is no physical reason to do so. Many physicians

have noticed that some patients die soon after receiving a negative prognosis, long before they were likely to die from the illness itself. In one case, a young man involved in a drug trial took an overdose (29 capsules) of what he thought was an anti-depressant and became dangerously ill. When he was told that he had been in the control group, taking a harmless placebo, he rapidly got better. There have even been suggestions that the health warnings on cigarette packages could make cigarettes more dangerous.

Chapter 2

What drives you?

The first aim of the brain is to help you survive.
After that, it pursues other needs.

Why do you do the things that you do? There are many different motivators. You make breakfast because you are hungry, and go to work because you need the money. But when you have satisfied basic needs, you probably move on to doing things that you think will make you happy.

Maslow's pyramid

In 1954, the American psychologist Abraham Maslow published a diagram that he claimed explained human motivation. The 'pyramid of needs' shows a hierarchy of needs that, he said, must be met in order. Trying to meet these needs provides, according to Maslow, the motivation for all human endeavour. When one need has been met, we move our sights on to the next in order.

Fed and watered

At the bottom of Maslow's pyramid are the most fundamental physical needs – the need for food, water, sleep, air and basic bodily functions (including sex, interestingly). Once these basic needs have been met, people progress to trying to satisfy the need for security. This is not just physical safety but the feeling of security that comes from having a stable job, a house that won't be repossessed, and a reasonable degree of confidence that you aren't going to drop dead of a heart attack at any minute (as Maslow did).

Although psychologists have largely moved on from Maslow's pyramid, it is still widely referred to in business studies and sociology.

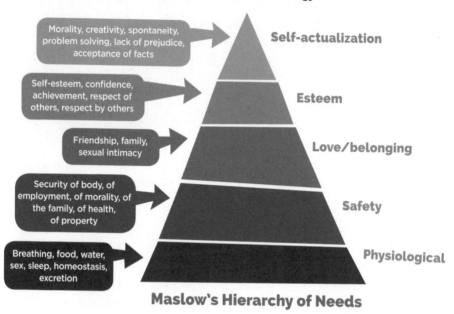

Morality, creativity, spontaneity, problem solving, lack of prejudice, acceptance of facts → **Self-actualization**

Self-esteem, confidence, achievement, respect of others, respect by others → **Esteem**

Friendship, family, sexual intimacy → **Love/belonging**

Security of body, of employment, of morality, of the family, of health, of property → **Safety**

Breathing, food, water, sex, sleep, homeostasis, excretion → **Physiological**

Maslow's Hierarchy of Needs

You and them

Following security, we can move on to needs that relate more to our place in relation to others. The need for love and belonging is met by having family, friends and (again) sexual intimacy. Celibate nuns and monks don't stand much chance in Maslow's world.

MASLOW'S HUMANISTIC PSYCHOLOGY

Abraham Maslow (1908–70) was born in New York, the youngest of seven children. He was classified as mentally unstable, suffered from anti-Semitic prejudice and bullying and had a very difficult relationship with a mother he neither liked nor respected. Later, he worked at Columbia University with psychologist Alfred Adler (one of Sigmund Freud's early colleagues), who became a mentor to him. Maslow became determined to work on the psychology of the healthy mind, rather than following the more usual path of psychopathology – working to understand and remedy disorders of the psyche. He set out to discover what motivates people, what are the sources and impulses of personal strength and fulfilment – a study he called 'humanistic psychology'. His work on the hierarchy of needs, self-actualization and peak experiences has been highly influential.

The next level is the need to be well regarded by others. This is esteem and respect, including self-esteem and confidence. Hermits and recluses who have no dealings with others need not apply.

The pinnacle of the pyramid is 'self-actualization' at which point

NEEDS AND WANTS

The difference between needs and wants is that needs are quantifiable and finite and wants are not. Once our basic needs are met, we can move on to another goal – so once we have enough air, food and water, we don't need lots more. (Although we might like a different type of food, or an extra pudding, we don't need it.) Wants are infinite. We might want a mobile phone, but then when we have one we want a better one, or we also want a camera, or a big car. Wants are insatiable, as there are always more popping up, like two new heads on a decapitated hydra.

STOICS AND CYNICS

The philosophical movements of cynicism and Stoicism, along with some Eastern religions, plot a path to tranquillity, enlightenment or self-actualization that detours around many of the 'needs' that Maslow said had to be met. Indeed, they tend towards the belief that fulfilment comes from rising above (rather than meeting) needs. The person who can learn to be untroubled by unmet needs will enjoy a more tranquil and satisfying life than one who is always struggling for the next promotion, the bigger TV and the larger expense account.

people are fulfilled and have become the people they want to be (see Chapter 15 – *Are you the best 'you' that you can be?* Page 160).

Acts and motivation

Maslow proposed that it is the hierarchy of needs that motivates human behaviour. If we are hungry, we will seek first of all to eat. If we don't have enough sleep, that will rule our behaviour as we try to secure time and space to rest. Once one tier of needs is met, we are motivated to satisfy the next tier of needs. Maslow claimed that we can't deal

The Greek philosopher Diogenes shunned property, living almost naked in an abandoned jar in the marketplace and eating scraps given to him by others. He was so self-actualized that Alexander the Great is said to have remarked that if he could not be Alexander, he would like to be Diogenes.

You might think you need a smart phone to live efficiently – but is it just a misplaced attempt to satisfy a need for esteem and identity?

with these needs out of sequence – we can only progress to needing, say, job security once we have enough food and water.

Only when all the lower needs are met can we look to meet the need for self-actualization. As a consequence, since many people aren't able to meet the lower needs, very few of us – perhaps as few as 1 or 2 per cent – will ever be self-actualized. That's rather a depressing prospect, which must have disappointed Maslow, who had intended to sort out the happy side of psychology.

But is it all true?

What's new?

For millennia, philosophy and religion had pitted the impulses that Maslow identified as higher needs against those he

Mortification of the flesh does not, according to Maslow's thinking, free the mind to focus on higher things, but chains it more securely to the needs of the body. He would say that we're more likely to achieve intellectual fulfilment in a cosy jumper than in a hairshirt.

called lower needs. The central dynamic between them was one of conflict, not progression. Maslow was unusual in acknowledging the importance – even primacy – of the needs that the likes of Diogenes wanted to deny or suppress. For Maslow, greater things became possible when physical needs were met rather than shunned.

Who, when, where?

Maslow drew up his hierarchy of needs after studying and considering a limited sample of people. The hierarchy is biased towards the concerns of white male Americans. Working from Maslow's rules, Jesus Christ would not have achieved self-actualization – he fell at the first hurdle, being born in a stable to poor parents and committed to chastity. More generally, Maslow's hierarchy is not applicable to very different cultures or societies in different times and places. America of the 1950s was an individualistic society. How would his pyramid have fared in a collectivist society, in which people are geared towards not their personal development but the good of the family group or society as a whole?

It is quite clear that even in an individualistic society, some of the needs can be leap-frogged and people can still reach self-actualization. There have been countless creative people who have lived in poverty or sickness, with no social or physical security, and

'Don't Stop Me Now' was recorded a line at a time because of Freddie Mercury's state of health – yet it is the ultimate paean to self-actualization.

yet have been able to produce wonderful work. Beethoven was deaf, Solzhenitsyn was in prison, Marie Curie was dying of radiation sickness and Freddie Mercury of AIDS when they did some of their greatest work. Adversity can even be a spur to self-actualization.

Some studies comparing perception of needs in the USA and the Middle East, in wartime and peacetime, threw up significant differences in prioritizing of needs. Some needs change with age, too – children prioritize physical needs and the need for love, and adolescents and young adults become more concerned with esteem.

More pyramids or fewer?

Maslow's pyramid was expanded during the 1960s and 1970s to seven or even eight levels. The new levels were cognitive and aesthetic needs, which were slotted in below self-actualization, and transcendence needs (very 1960s), which was placed in the tier above. Cognitive needs are the requirement for knowledge and meaning; aesthetic needs relate to an appreciation of beauty, form and balance. Transcendence covers fostering self-actualization in others.

ERG-onomics

The American psychologist Clayton Paul Alderfer (born 1940) developed Maslow's pyramid slightly differently, categorizing the needs as promoting existence, relatedness and growth (ERG). Alderfer saw the lowest level in Maslow's scheme as relating to physical 'existence'. He classified the needs that had to do with a place in society and

SEX AND VIOLENCE HELD IN CHECK

Sigmund Freud, the father of psychoanalysis, divided the psyche into three levels: the id, the ego and the super-ego. The id was unrestrained instincts, passions and hungers, lusting after sexual gratification and a good fight. It was kept in order by the ego, which negotiated the id's way through the world to avoid too much conflict. The super-ego was something like the conscience and could prevent some of the more outlandish promptings of the id coming to fruition. The id, then, is the main motivating force and the ego and super-ego keep it in check.

relationships with others as 'relatedness'. The need for self-esteem and self-actualization he labelled 'growth'.

Alderfer made a place in his scheme for regression. If a higher-level need is not met, the individual will slip down the ladder and make redoubled efforts at a lower need in the hope of satisfying a higher need. We can see this every day in people who think they will be satisfied and happy if they earn more and spend more on assorted 'stuff'. The attempt to fulfil spiritual needs through the acquisition of physical goods is doomed to failure.

It's all good

While some psychologists were shoe-horning new tiers into Maslow's pyramid, others were keen to demolish it. In its place came systems that proposed a more horizontal plane of needs.

The Chilean-born German economist and environmentalist Manfred Max-Neef has proposed a taxonomy of human needs that he sees as being inter-related and interdependent. He classifies human needs as:

• subsistence • protection • affection • understanding
• participation • leisure • creation • identity • freedom.

By fitting them into categories of being (qualities), having (things), doing (actions) and interacting (settings) he developed a matrix of thirty-six items.

These fundamental human needs don't have to be satisfied in

CAN'T GET NO SATISFACTION

Clearly Max-Neef had a considerable personal need for classifying things as he also went on to classify six types of 'satisfier' or method of meeting (or failing to meet) needs. These are:

• Violators: these claim to satisfy a need, but actually make the situation worse. An example would be carrying a weapon to satisfy a need for personal security.

• Pseudo-satisfiers: these claim to satisfy a need, but actually have little or no real effect. An example might be dressing in designer clothes to give yourself a sense of belonging and identity, whereas the identity belongs to the clothes, not to you.

• Inhibiting satisfiers: these over-satisfy one need, and consequently make it harder to satisfy other needs. If parents are over-attentive, for instance, they make it hard for their child to develop independence and a security that is rooted in their own sense of responsibility.

• Singular satisfiers: these satisfy a single need and have no impact on others. For example, providing food assistance to people who are hungry helps to satisfy their need for food, but doesn't address the need for housing or heating or improve their future prospects for food security. Government and charitable programmes often fall into this category.

• Synergistic satisfiers: these satisfy a specific need and also help to meet other needs. For example, providing nutritious, free school meals gives a child food, but also helps to build knowledge about healthy eating and nurtures a sense of community.

Breastfeeding is a synergistic satisfier: it provides the baby with nourishment, but also enhanced disease immunity, affection, closeness and bonding, and develops attachment (see Chapter 6: Does indulgence spoil a baby? Page 73).

any particular order, and the satisfaction of some will go some way towards the satisfaction of others. They don't form a hierarchy, but for a society to flourish people have to feel all these needs are being met. Satisfying these needs gives a community a way of identifying and measuring its 'wealths' and 'poverties'.

Got what you need?

The first step to meeting our needs is to identify them. Unless we opt for one of the wholesale schemas, such as Maslow's hierarchy or Max-Neef's taxonomy, we need to work out for ourselves what our goals are. That's easier said than done, as the massive market in self-help publications demonstrates. For many people, the real goal is to be happy. But how to achieve it?

Chapter 3

Don't you have a mind of your own?

You might believe you know what you think – but most of us are easily swayed to change our ideas.

Imagine this: you're watching a TV talent show and everyone else is rooting for the performer you hate. Are you going to buck the trend and criticize the favourite? Or will you go with the flow, maybe even deciding the guy's not so bad really? After all, if all your friends like his act, perhaps you're missing something...

Psychology experiments suggest we are often less resistant to the pressure to conform than we might believe. We will go along with other people's views even when there is no material cost in not conforming. Just why are you putty in their hands?

The Asch conformity experiment

In 1951, the Polish-born social psychologist Solomon Asch (1907–96) carried out a groundbreaking experiment in conformity at Swarthmore College, Pennsylvania. In the main part of the experiment, a subject was placed with seven people who were presented as volunteers but who were actually confederates of Asch working to an agreed script.

The group was shown two cards. One displayed a single line. The other showed three lines of differing lengths, one of which matched the line on the first card. The group was asked to say which of the three lines, labelled A, B and C, matched the single line. This was repeated many times. For the first set of trials, Asch's confederates gave the correct answer. Thereafter, they all gave the same wrong answer. All the confederates gave their answers first, leaving the volunteer last to give a response each time. Asch was interested to see whether volunteers would be swayed by the wrong answers given by others.

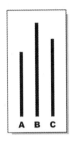

Subjects in Asch's experiment had to say which line on the right-hand card matched the line on the left-hand card.

In a control experiment, a volunteer had to give answers without other people being present and therefore with no pressure to conform. In the control, the volunteer gave an incorrect answer less than 1 per cent of the time. This showed that the task was not especially difficult.

In the genuine trials, volunteers gave wrong answers 33 per cent of the time when the confederates also gave the wrong answer, with 75 per cent of volunteers giving a wrong answer at least once. Asch then interviewed participants and explained the true nature of the experiment. He noted how they explained their behaviour.

Along the right lines?

People who conformed to the group answer, whether or not it was correct, might have:

- actually believed the incorrect answer was true – relatively few fell into this group

- reached a point where they realized they must be wrong as everyone else agreed on a different answer – Asch called this a 'distortion of judgment'
- realized everyone else was giving the wrong answer, but agreed with it so as not to be the odd one out or look inferior – Asch called this a 'distortion of action'.

More people decided that they must be wrong if everyone else agreed, putting them in the 'distortion of judgment' group.

Among those who did not conform to the consensus, people might:

- act confidently in disagreeing, even though they felt some conflict
- act in a withdrawn way, with no conflict
- show doubt, but still give the answer they thought was true as they felt the need to do the task properly.

Join the club – for a while

In variations on his experiment, Asch discovered that there was less conformity if a single other person gave the correct response, or if subjects were allowed to record their own response in writing rather than make it public. This suggests that they didn't want to look foolish to other participants by giving the 'wrong' answer, rather than that they struggled either to know the answer or to represent to themselves that they disagreed with the majority verdict.

Asch cited his experimental results as evidence of normative social influence – that is, that people tend to conform publicly to the majority decision or view in order to be accepted by the group, even though they might privately disagree or reject a view. But the social psychologist John Turner argued that the participants revealed in the interviews that they did have genuine uncertainty about the correct answer. The answer might have been obvious to the researchers, but it need not have been so to the participants (though looking at the cards, it's hard to see how people could have genuinely got the answer wrong). Did they really doubt the answer, or were they trying to persuade themselves that they did because they preferred to see themselves as poor at comparing lines rather than as conforming to a bad decision? John Turner developed self-categorization theory, which deals with how we see ourselves, and how we interpret our own actions.

Peer pressure

Asch's experiment dealt with peer pressure. This is the pressure we all feel (and many respond to) to conform to the norms in our social group. It's not just advertising that makes you buy a particular brand of smart phone or trainers. You are also swayed if people around you have them. If all those discerning people – in the social group you respect, belong to, or aspire to join – chose a particular product, surely they must be right? Peer pressure is supposed to explain why young people take up smoking, underage sex and cyberbullying.

Advertisers promote an image of successful/attractive/intelligent people 'like you' buying and using their products so that even if the people around you aren't actually using them, you will consider yourself an outsider unless you conform. You're an attractive, intelligent person, aren't you? So why don't you have the watch, mobile phone, or car that is the badge of your tribe? It takes some self-confidence to buy a cheap, inelegant mobile phone when everyone else you know owns the latest sleek model. Peer pressure is harnessed deliberately and cynically in other areas of life, too.

Employers hold bonding exercises such as weekend survival camps, parties and other social events that foster the belief in employees that they are among friends, not just work colleagues. If you feel as though you belong to a group in which the other members turn up early and work hard, it's likely that you will do the same.

No big deal

The Asch experiment wasn't sinister. It didn't require participants to do anything immoral or even particularly uncomfortable. The worst a non-conformist could expect was ridicule from people he didn't know, and the worst a conformist could experience was embarrassment when the true nature of the experiment was revealed. But it's the thin end of the wedge. It's easy to underestimate

PEER PRESSURE – WHO'S PRESSING WHOM?

When we think of peer pressure, we tend to imagine 'peers' putting pressure on someone to do something – smoke a cigarette, for instance, or drink alcohol. That does happen, but more often the pressure comes from ourselves. We want to be part of the group that does dangerous stunts or takes party drugs because those people are cool and we want to be seen as cool and to see ourselves as cool. Internal pressure is more compelling than external pressure – and potentially much more dangerous.

the power of peer pressure. How far will people go in order to conform, to be part of a tribe? It seems they will do things they previously considered unthinkable.

The Third Wave

In 1967, in Palo Alto, California, history teacher Ron Jones was having a hard time persuading his high school students that fascism could have taken root so securely and quickly in Nazi Germany. To their credit, the students found it hard to believe that ordinary, intelligent German citizens could have bought into an ideology that led to the gas chambers and an ambition to create a 10,000-year Reich. Unable to get them to accept it using his usual teaching methods, Jones decided to show them.

He started a movement, which he called the Third Wave, that had the aim of overthrowing democracy. You might think that aim in itself would alienate the students, but he made a convincing case for a different system being better able to deliver a high standard of performance and so greater rewards for individuals. The problem with democracy, he said, is that because it focuses on the individual, it reduces the strength of the group.

A slippery slope

On the first day, he insisted that students stand up to ask or answer a question, open each remark by addressing him as 'Mr Jones', sit according to his seating plan and follow strict discipline in class. Acting as an authoritarian figure, he improved the efficiency of the class considerably. Originally, he had intended to stop the experiment after the first day. But it was going well, so he took it a bit further.

> *'Strength through discipline, strength through community, strength through action, strength through pride.'*
> Motto of Jones' Third Wave group

The second day, he introduced a salute and demanded that students greet each other with it even outside class. They all complied. The group developed quite astonishing coherence and self-discipline. People like to belong, and the more special belonging seems, the more they want it. By the third day, the 'movement' had spread beyond the history class with other students asking to join. The academic performance and motivation of all members improved dramatically. Jones assigned members individual tasks, such as designing a banner, and showed them how to initiate new members. He told them to exclude non-members from his classroom. By the end of the third day, there were two hundred members (it had started with only the thirty members of Jones' class). Some members spontaneously started reporting any members who breached the many rules. It had become a self-policing movement.

All the way down

On the fourth day, Jones felt the experiment was getting out of hand and decided to end it. He told all members that the movement was part of a national movement that would be announced the next day and that they were to attend a rally at noon to watch a broadcast by the movement's presidential candidate. When they turned up, he told them that they had been part of an experiment in fascism and had all willingly – and rapidly – welded themselves into a group convinced of their own superiority. Then he showed them a film about Nazi Germany. Touché.

So who do you think you are?

According to psychologist Wendy Treynor, the 'identity shift effect' is at work when we give in to peer pressure. To start with, we fear social rejection if our behaviour doesn't match the standard behaviour of the group. When we adjust our behaviour to fit in, we

Thousands of books smoulder in a huge bonfire as Germans give the Nazi salute.

feel uncomfortable because our behaviour now doesn't match our own beliefs or standards. This is cognitive dissonance (see page 263). To get rid of the internal conflict, we adjust our standards to match those we have just adopted. This returns us to the harmonious state of no conflict, either internal or external, and the happy state of fitting in with our peers. Everyone is happy. But sometimes they are happy Nazis.

Chapter 4

All for one or one for all?

Are we naturally selfish or generous? Or is being generous just another way of being selfish?

If left to our own devices, would we all be kind to one another or brutish and selfish? Psychologists and philosophers have argued the case for either position. Biology, and the principle of the selfish gene, could argue it either way – it's good for you, as an individual, to further your own cause and that of your family (your genes); but for the species as a whole, it's better if we cooperate and are kind to one another.

> *'She is such a good friend that she would throw all her acquaintances into the water for the pleasure of fishing them out again.'*
> Charles Maurice de Talleyrand (1754–1838)

Wild humans

If we could investigate humans 'in the wild' we could examine innate behaviour without the crust of social niceties laid down over millennia. But we can't, and even 20th-century anthropologists who studied non-industrialized societies were still looking at societies with rules that either reinforced or obscured what might be natural behaviour.

Even so, humans are animals, and we can look at other animals to see whether empathy and selflessness are naturally occurring traits. If other animals are naturally helpful, even altruistic, perhaps people are, too.

Are rats kinder than you?

We tend to think of rats as dirty, disease-carrying and vicious. But they are (also) smart and altruistic. A study in 1958 found that if

KICKED OUT OF THE CAVE?

If human beings naturally had an 'all for one' attitude, we would expect individuals who were no longer functionally useful to be excluded from societies with scarce resources. Yet evidence suggests this is not the case. Remains of prehistoric cave dwellers have been discovered with signs of severe injuries or disabilities that would have prevented them from gathering or preparing food, or performing other essential tasks. Some have clearly been cared for into old age, or for a considerable time after their disability occurred.

The skeleton of a disabled prehistoric man found in North Vietnam. Archaeologists have concluded that he would have had little, if any, use of his arms and would have been unable to feed himself. He could only have survived into adulthood by being cared for by other members of his community.

A man in his twenties, buried in North Vietnam 4,000 years ago, had severe disabilities, caused by a genetic condition that would have started in adolescence. That he had survived for another ten years proved that others had cared for him even though he could not contribute to the community. The 45,000-year-old skeleton of a severely disabled man found in Iraq, and the skull of a brain-damaged child who lived in Spain 530,000 years ago, show that 'care in the community' goes back a very long way.

pressing a lever to get food gave an electric shock to another rat, rats would go hungry.

A more sophisticated study in 1967 explored this further. A cage had two levers for delivering food, one that was easy to operate and one that was very difficult to operate. Sensibly, the rats used the easy one. But when the system was changed so that a second group of rats received an electric shock when that lever was used, the rats cooperated to work the difficult lever together.

In 2011, a study in Chicago found the altruism of rats to go even further. Offered the choice of operating a lever to free a trapped rat, or eating chocolate, the rats freed the trapped rat. They then shared the chocolate. The rats could have eaten the chocolate first and then freed the other rat, but chose the sharing option.

Is altruism good for you?

Monkeys spend a lot of time grooming one another. This apparent act of kindness has obvious benefits for the community. It helps to build bonds between individuals, making the community stronger. It reduces the parasite population, making the community healthier and benefiting each individual. But there is more to it than that.

Some scientists have suggested that altruism in animals (and humans) can make an individual look attractive to a mate. Not only are they kind, but they have resources to spare. A partner with time to spare to groom his siblings must be good at finding food.

Stuart Semple of Roehampton University, London, studied grooming and stress in Barbary macaque monkeys. He found that monkeys who groom others have lower stress levels than those who don't. It could be that being totally laid-back and stress-free makes the monkeys more likely to groom their

'Do not hide behind such superficialities as whether you should or should not give a dime to a beggar. That is not the issue. The issue is whether you do or do not have the right to exist without giving him that dime. The issue is whether you must keep buying your life, dime by dime, from any beggar who might choose to approach you. The issue is whether the need of others is the first mortgage on your life and the moral purpose of your existence. The issue is whether man is to be regarded as a sacrificial animal. Any man of self-esteem will answer: "No." Altruism says: "Yes."'
Ayn Rand, 1960

neighbours, rather than that the grooming reduces stress – we can't be sure of cause and effect without more research.

So, altruism is selfish?

Possibly. Helping others makes us feel good. It also makes other people admire us. Some people avoid social admiration by giving anonymously, but they still get personal satisfaction from doing good. They might even get extra satisfaction out of shunning public acclaim.

In terms of survival of a species, altruism is useful, so it would be beneficial for evolution to have made us feel good when we are generous. Just don't feel you can occupy the moral high ground with too much fervour when you do it, because we know you enjoy it really.

There have been many reports of dolphins aiding those in trouble at sea, helping to keep swimmers afloat, and scaring away sharks that come to attack them. They have also been known to guide stranded whales back to deep water.

Chapter 5

Who cares what celebrities think?

Just because someone can sing doesn't mean they understand politics or anything else.

Singers are famous and successful because they can sing well, actors because they can act well, sports(wo)men because they can play sport well and models because they are good-looking. If you want an example of how to sing, act, play sport or look good, you can't beat them. But why do we care what they think about politics, charity, child-rearing, dieting, cooking or any of the other issues so many of them dabble in or pronounce upon?

It's called the 'halo effect'.

He seems a nice man

In 1920, American psychologist Edward Thorndike published his findings on how commanding officers rated the soldiers in their charge. The COs had to assess them on physical qualities (such as neatness, voice and bearing), intellect, leadership skills, and personal qualities (including dependability, loyalty and selflessness). The officers tended to find them either good across the board, or pretty bad at just about everything. There were few instances of COs rating soldiers well on some attributes and badly on others.

It seems that we have a tendency to generalize from one attribute to others, so a positive opinion of someone is likely to extend to all areas of their personality. Conversely, if we take against someone, we will assume that they are bad through and through. This not only includes related traits (if someone is mean and selfish, it might seem reasonable to assume they will be unhelpful and stingy) but also extends to unrelated aspects (such as assuming that as they are selfish they are also lacking

> *'What planet is he living on?'*
> President Mitterand of France, talking about Ronald Reagan

VOTE REAGAN – BUT WHY?

Many actors have become politicians. Some have been genuinely intelligent people and made good politicians. On some, the jury is still out. In other cases, their performance was unremittingly poor. During his time in office as US president, Ronald Reagan was mocked for his evident stupidity and laziness, caught sleeping through important conferences on several occasions, and recorded giving information that was so inaccurate it was laughable. Yet these traits were also clear when he was governor of California and he was still proposed and voted president. Why? Because people liked his films, his familiarity and his manner – so they assumed he would be a good president. As it turned out, under Reagan the US enjoyed a period of economic prosperity and national security with low unemployment and the end of the Cold War. California was also buoyant when he was governor (unlike under Arnold Schwarzenegger, another actor). Not all actors make bad politicians, of course. But voting for someone on the basis of being a good actor isn't a sound strategy.

in intelligence). It's a tendency that can even mix physical and psychological attributes. For example, disliking someone's voice or accent, or finding them either physically attractive or repellent, can affect how we view their character.

Would you buy underwear from David Beckham?

Advertisers rely on the halo effect when they use celebrities to endorse their products. Some endorsements make sense: if a successful athlete advertises trainers there is good reason to suppose he might know a good trainer when he sees one. (Though it's more likely he just knows a good million dollars when he sees one.) But why would we share his taste in underwear?

Similarly, why would a beautiful young model, too young to have wrinkles,

endorse a good wrinkle cream?

Advertisers always work on aspiration and association – we see an attractive person in a glamorous setting using a product and buy into the implication that some of that glamour will rub off on us if we use the same product. Celebrity endorsement goes further than that, though, in that it trades on our subconscious assumption that if someone is good at singing/acting/kicking a ball, they will also have sound judgement when it comes to choosing breakfast cereal/cars/underwear.

> *'In one study, men who saw a new-car ad that included a seductive young woman model rated the car as faster, more appealing, more expensive-looking, and better designed than did men who viewed the same ad without the model. Yet when asked later, the men refused to believe that the presence of the young woman had influenced their judgments.'*
> Robert Cialdini, Arizona State University

The good impression created by the product's association with the celebrity is 'sticky' – we will remember it even if we know nothing else about the product, and so be more likely to choose it. Of course, the opposite is also true – if we dislike the celebrity, we will be less likely to choose the product. That's why only physically attractive and inoffensive celebrities are generally chosen to appear in advertisements and why advertisers are quick to drop celebrities who become embroiled in embarrassing scandals.

First impressions count

First impressions are notoriously difficult to change. If you make a bad impression the first time you meet someone, it's hard to get them to think well of you. And if you like someone straight off, they have to do something seriously bad before you turn against them.

We don't like being wrong or admitting we're wrong. And revising our first impressions involves admitting to ourselves that we were wrong in our initial assessment. We'd actually rather spend time with someone we now know is not very nice than admit we were wrong in judging them to be nice in the first place. The more time and emotional energy we invest in someone, the harder it is to admit we were wrong about them.

He couldn't have done it

When a celebrity is accused of a horrible crime, there is often a knee-jerk reaction among the public to denounce the denouncement. But a lot depends on the public image the celebrity had previously projected. When the movie director Woody Allen was accused of abuse by his adopted daughter in 2014, many people with no

The extent of the child abuse carried out by British music presenter Jimmy Savile was only uncovered after his death. His popularity as a performer and his work for charity made him immune from suspicion and investigation during his lifetime – even when the signs were clearly visible. The 'culture of abuse' within the BBC could endure only because of the halo effect.

personal knowledge of the individuals or the case leapt to conclusions about his innocence or guilt. Those who assumed his daughter was lying based their view on their admiration for him as a film director. (As many people assumed he was guilty, for equally unfounded reasons, but not based on the halo effect.)

The same assumptions protect many people in high office and positions of public trust. Just because someone has a good political brain it doesn't mean he or she will also be moral in their sexual behaviour, honest in their dealings with their employees or kind to their children. The word of a non-famous person (such as children abused by

CAN YOU STILL LIKE THEIR WORK?

Eric Gill, a brilliant typeface designer, sexually abused his own children, had an incestuous relationship with his sister and had sex with his dog.

Roman Polanski, director of *Rosemary's Baby* and *Tess*, can't return to the USA as he is still wanted for the rape of a minor. He skipped bail just before sentencing in 1977 and fled to France. The poet Ezra Pound was an anti-Semitic Nazi sympathizer with a wife and a mistress who had children by both of them.

Composer Richard Wagner (above right) was famed for his anti-Semitic views, and Carl Orff was a Nazi sympathizer. Edward Thorndike (right), who identified the halo effect, was an influential psychologist who promoted eugenics.

Jimmy Savile, left) carries little weight with the public and so is more likely to be disbelieved.

Tainted love

It makes us uneasy to like the art of creators who led disreputable personal lives. If we know an artist beat or betrayed his wife, was cruel to his children, was racist, or fascist, it can make us feel uncomfortable about their work – even if they're dead and so not going to get any money or gratification from our liking them. It's the opposite of the halo effect, with our dislike of one aspect of them tainting others.

Pretty and good, or just pretty good?

Physically attractive people have advantages over average-looking people in many arenas. They are more likely to get a job, to have favours done for them and even to receive favourable treatment by the legal system if they commit a crime (unless they used their attractiveness to commit the crime, such as to deceive people). In 2013, Italian researchers submitted fake job applications using photos of both attractive and unattractive people, with identical employment records. The attractive people were more likely to be called for interviews than the unattractive people. The average interviewing rate was 30 per cent. Attractive women received interview requests 54 per cent of the time, and attractive men 47 per cent of the time.

On the whole, attractive people earn 10–15 per cent more over their lifetimes than those with average looks. Daniel Hamermesh at the University of Texas has calculated that, for the less-than-average-looking person, this amounts to around $140,000 (£89,000) in lost income. He has proposed that legislation should be brought in to protect the aesthetically challenged from being discriminated against on the grounds of their appearance.

Chapter 6

Does indulgence spoil a baby?

Should you leave a baby to cry or give comfort?
Which is better for the baby?

Trends in baby-care come and go. Sometimes, the professionals tell parents to leave babies to cry, to avoid giving them too much attention, to feed them on a strict four-hour regime and basically let them know who's boss (and it's not the baby!). At other times, they tell parents to be led by the baby, feeding on demand, fitting around the baby's sleep patterns, engaging fully and frequently with the baby with lots of hugs, talking, attention and playing. Is it just fashion? Or is there a right way? And can the 'right' way be right for both baby and parent, or is it simply a matter of deciding who to prioritize?

> *'When you are tempted to pet your child, remember that mother love is a dangerous instrument. An instrument which may inflict a never-healing wound, a wound which may make infancy unhappy, adolescence a nightmare, an instrument which may wreck your adult son or daughter's vocational future and their chances for marital happiness.*
>
> *'Never, never kiss your child. Never hold it in your lap. Never rock its carriage.'*
> John B. Watson, 1928

Brutal regime

In the first half of the 20th century, the 'experts' in child psychology and child-rearing were generally of the opinion that childhood and motherly love were unnecessary indulgences. 'We need less sentimentality and more spanking,' said Granville Stanley Hall, pioneer of child psychology and first president of the American Psychological Association. (Despite his credentials, he was a eugenicist who thought no effort should be made to help the physically or mentally ill or disabled, as this was standing in the way of evolution.)

'Less sentimentality and more spanking' was a view shared by many, and parents were generally encouraged to prioritize discipline over affection towards even the youngest children. This was the age in which the wealthy sent their children away to private boarding schools, when cold showers and a good beating were considered character-building, and many parents were emotionally distant – either because they believed it to be beneficial or because they found it convenient.

Many children of wealthy families in the early 20th century rarely saw their parents, being looked after by nannies and forming their strongest emotional attachments with domestic staff.

Attachment theory

It was against this background that British psychologist John Bowlby studied attachment in small children.

Bowlby collected observational data on

institutionalized and delinquent children or children who had been separated from their parents or orphaned in the war. As there were no theories on which to base his conclusions about attachment, Bowlby looked at studies in ethnology, evolution and animal behaviour. He considered Konrad Lorenz's work on imprinting in birds in the 1930s to be highly relevant (see panel). He developed the theory that there are sound evolutionary reasons for babies to form a close attachment with one individual – usually the mother. Infants that bond closely with a parent and are therefore looked after and protected by that parent have a better chance of growing up and having children of their own. The infant has behaviours – crying and smiling, for instance – that encourage the parent to interact. It is the parent's instinct, produced through

MOTHER GOOSE

Austrian zoologist Konrad Lorenz studied the 'imprinting' behaviour of newly-hatched greylag geese. This behaviour leads them to form an attachment with the first suitable object they see. In nature, the first thing they see will be the parent, and the gosling will sensibly follow the parent's lead and learn how to be a goose. Lorenz imprinted goslings on himself (or, rather his boots – they would follow anyone wearing the boots) and was often followed around by a troupe of goslings. It was cute, but probably not very good for the geese.

evolution, to respond to these stimuli from the baby.

Bowlby suspected that ignoring the stimuli and refusing interaction, as the brutalist school of parenting recommended, could do irreparable damage to the child as it prevented the formation of a primary attachment. Children who grow up without a primary attachment can later suffer, he claimed, from delinquency, depression, reduced

By imprinting orphaned or endangered birds on microlight aircraft, they can be taught their natural migratory paths, something they otherwise would not know without parental guidance.

intelligence and 'affectionless psychopathy' (meaning they act without regard for the emotional impact on others).

Now or never

Bowlby believed there was a critical period during which attachment must be established and maintained. If the child did not form and sustain a bond with a primary care-giver in the first two years of life, it would be unable to do so later on. He said that for these first two years the child should receive continuous care from the primary attachment figure, who was usually the mother (at least in the 1940s and 1950s when he was carrying out his research). His recommendation has implications for children attending day-care or being looked after by other carers. Indeed, he claimed the risk from breaking the primary attachment continued until age five, and that included separation from and death of the care-giver.

THE 'FORTY-FOUR THIEVES'

Bowlby conducted a study to test his theory of attachment. He interviewed forty-four young people in a child guidance clinic who had been convicted of burglary, and forty-four other children (the control group) who were attending the clinic but had no criminal convictions. He found that of the forty-four thieves, more than 80 per cent had been separated from their mother for more than six months during their early life, and more than 30 per cent showed signs of affectionless psychopathy. Of the control group, only a small proportion had been separated from their mothers, and none showed psychopathy.

Critics of Bowlby's study point out that the separation was self-reported and the information could have been inaccurate. In addition, Bowlby conducted the interviews and determined the presence or absence of psychopathy himself, so his interpretation might have been biased in favour of his theory ('experimenter bias').

During the early years, the child learns how to be a person from interaction with the mother or other primary attachment, internalizing a model of how to be in the world. The most important lessons, which will last a lifetime, are that:

- others are trustworthy
- the child is a valuable person
- the child can effectively interact with others.

Around the age of three, these lessons – or the form of them that emerges from the individual child's primary attachment – become internalized into a working model that the child will draw on forever (or until expensive therapy tries to remedy any deficits).

WHO cares

Following his work on attachment in the 1940s, Bowlby was asked by the World Health Organization (WHO) to report on the mental health of homeless children in post-war Europe. His publication, *Maternal Care and Mental Health* (1951), changed the way orphans and displaced children were considered and cared for.

At the same time, public opinion was undergoing a sea change, brought about by the groundbreaking work of Dr Benjamin Spock. *The Common Sense Book of Baby and Child Care* (1946) overturned the conventional wisdom of beating children into submission, and recommended paying attention to them and

giving them love and affection. It went on to become a worldwide best-seller, with more than fifty million copies sold.

It seems inconceivable to most parents now that anyone would have followed a strict regime of leaving a hungry baby to cry until the allocated feeding time, but apparently post-war parents needed the permission of Dr Spock before they would employ the common-sense practices of feeding hungry babies and comforting sad babies. Although some of Spock's practical baby care advice has been superseded (current advice is not to place babies on their stomachs, as he recommends), the emotional

SPOCK BACKLASH

When the Spock babies grew up, the world changed. The sexual permissiveness of the 1960s, the drug-using hippies, the Civil Rights movement, the opposition to the Vietnam War and capitalism, and the rejection of the 1950s *Stepford Wives* lifestyle were all laid at the door of Dr Spock. Did permissive parenting produce the criticized excesses of the 'me' generation?

and psychological approach is still very influential.

What Bowlby got wrong

Few people would now dispute that a child benefits immensely from receiving loving care and attention from at least one stable figure during infancy. But some of the details of Bowlby's conclusions have come under fire.

> '*The U.S. [paid] the price of two generations that followed the Dr. Spock baby plan of instant gratification of needs.*' Norman Vincent Peale, best-selling author of *The Power of Positive Thinking*

In talking about 'maternal deprivation', he does not distinguish between deprivation and privation. In deprivation, an attachment is established and then disrupted or removed. In privation, no attachment is formed at all. The latter is far more damaging to the child (see panel *The Romanian Orphanage Children*, page 86).

The type of distress that Bowlby noted as occurring when the infant was separated from the mother also occurs when the infant is separated from other significant figures in his or her life, such as the father, a sibling or other close relative or care-giver.

A study in 1964 found that the first significant individual attachment starts around eight months and others quickly follow. By eighteen months of age, many children have two, three, four or more attachments, and only 13 per cent had a single attachment.

In a further study of privation in 1981, Michael Rutter found that children who never formed a primary attachment were at first clingy, attention-seeking and indiscriminate in choosing people to befriend, and were later unable to follow rules, form relationships or feel guilt. But he argued that this was not necessarily a direct consequence of the lack of a mother-figure, as it could also be caused by being moved around a lot, having a poor diet, or any of the other factors that also distinguished the early lives of many of these children.

Milk isn't everything

The idea that the infant's primary need is not milk but affectionate physical contact flew in the face of all that was current in theories of

PSYCHOBABBLE: MONOTROPY

Monotropy is the attachment of an infant to a single adult, often the mother. It was central to Bowlby's model, but is not characteristic of all child-rearing practice. In Israeli kibbutzim, and in some totalitarian regimes and extremist religious groups, close attachment to a parent has been prevented by communal child-rearing. Some of the children, as adults, have spoken out against this method as being damaging. On the other hand, children can be happily reared with more than one strong attachment – two present and involved parents being the obvious model.

A CHILD GOES TO HOSPITAL

Bowlby and his colleague the social worker James Robertson promoted a film that Robertson made, called *A Two-Year-Old Goes to Hospital*. This documented the distress of a child who attended hospital for an operation without her mother in the early 1950s. The film prompted a major reform in paediatric care in hospitals and other state institutions.

childcare in the 1950s, but was endorsed by later research.

American psychologist Harry Harlow carried out an experiment designed specifically to test whether a mother means more to an infant than just a source of nourishment.

Wire mothers and fur mothers

Harlow's experiment would not be allowed now – but it revolutionized views on infancy, parental love and the psychological importance of affection. In 1958, Harlow took new-born rhesus monkeys from their mothers and placed them in cages, in isolation. They could hear and see other young monkeys, but not touch or interact with them. Initially, he was just raising the monkeys in the most efficient way for use in the laboratory. But he noticed that those hand-reared without interaction with other young monkeys or parents were psychologically very different from monkeys reared by their parents. He noticed, too, that in the absence of anything else soft, the babies clung to their cloth nappies. He set out to investigate the role of maternal presence and affection in child development.

Harlow made surrogate monkey mothers from wire and wood. Each baby monkey had its own surrogate mother, and grew attached to it, learning to recognize it and preferring it to other similar ones. He then created some that were bare wire frameworks and some that were covered with cloth. He put one of each in every monkey's cage. In each case, either the cloth mother was fitted with a feeding bottle, or the wire-frame mother held the bottle. The baby monkeys all preferred the cloth mothers, whether or not they provided food.

In the cages where the wire mothers provided the milk, babies went to the wire mothers only to suckle, then returned to the fabric mothers for comfort. If the baby monkeys were placed in a new environment with their surrogate fabric mothers, they would explore the environment, returning frequently to the fabric mother for comfort. If they were placed alone in the environment, they showed distress (such as curling up and screaming) and did not explore.

Harlow's conclusion – that nourishment is not by any means the most important aspect of the bond between mother and child – had a revolutionary impact.

A fork in the road

Today, baby care advice falls into two broad camps. Some professionals want to impose a strict schedule on young children (though it doesn't go as far as advocating 'less sentimentality and more spanking'). At the same time, the baby-led approach has gone even further towards putting the baby at the centre of his or her own care, with developments such as baby-led weaning, in which the child is never fed by a parent or carer but allowed to pick up, drop, throw or play with food at will.

Spock's encouragement to parents to trust and follow their instincts has rather fallen by the wayside as more and more 'experts' vie for the attention of parents, making them feel less and less confident in their instincts.

THE ROMANIAN ORPHANAGE CHILDREN

Under the regime of Nicolae Ceaușescu in Romania, up to 170,000 children were incarcerated in orphanages enduring neglect and abuse. Many were kept tied to their cots, lying in their own filth, and never picked up or shown affection. After the execution of Ceaușescu in 1989, their plight became known outside Romania and a number of charities moved in to help the orphans. Many of the orphans showed lasting effects from the deprivation they suffered. By the age of fifteen, some still looked to be around six or seven years old. Their brains failed to produce growth hormones. Many had impaired intelligence. These are the results not of malnutrition but of being deprived of intellectual

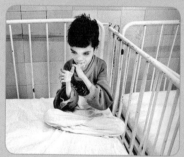

stimulation and emotional care. Many formed indiscriminate attachments and, if picked up, would howl and scream on being put down again. Some taken out of the orphanages at young ages and placed in loving foster homes made good progress, but for many the damage was irreparable.

In the late 1980s, children in Romanian orphanages were unable to form attachments with adults and suffered poor conditions and frequent ill-treatment. Children removed from the orphanages at a very young age often recovered, but others suffered lasting psychological damage.

Chapter 7

Is morality natural?

Do even very small children show a
sense of morality?

By the time children start school, they have developed a rudimentary sense of fairness and justice. They know which actions to classify as nice or nasty (or good or evil) and will loudly shout 'That's not fair!' at every opportunity (often when it is fair). Where do they get this sense from?

Start from home

In their early years, children are exposed to lots of behaviour in the real world, and on television and other media such as apps and movies. They witness adult responses to their own behaviour and that of others, and begin to learn about what is considered acceptable behaviour and what is unacceptable. But the work of Paul Bloom, a behavioural psychologist at Yale University, Connecticut,

suggests that observation and interaction are not the only elements involved.

Unlikely as it sounds, he has studied morality in babies as young as a few months old and concludes that our morality is not all learned from our dealings with others. His results offer the surprising suggestion that we have an innate moral sense, present even in the smallest infants. That moral sense is then fine-tuned as we grow, and is adjusted to suit the society into which we were born.

Moral relativism

Different types of behaviour have a different status in different communities. In the West it is now considered wrong to discriminate against someone on the basis of skin colour, for instance, yet for centuries that was regarded as acceptable behaviour. In Muslim countries, drinking alcohol is considered wrong and is forbidden. Some societies outlaw homosexuality. In major Western democracies the act of burning the national flag is considered wrong, as is ignoring the wishes of the dead. Some cultural groups consider it wrong to eat certain types of meat, or certain foods in combination. These types of moral behaviours are culture-specific and must be learned by each citizen.

'Everyone without exception believes his own native customs, and the religion he was brought up in, to be the best.'
Herodotus, *Histories*, 500BC

On the other hand, there is pretty much universal agreement about the morality or immorality of some acts. Most societies consider it wrong to commit murder, to steal from others, and to have sex with close blood relatives. As these moral strictures crop up in almost all societies, there might be something innate about them – or they might just evolve again and again as they make societies run smoothly.

Moral babies

Bloom's work with small babies shows, he says, that they exhibit a basic moral sense long before they are old enough to have learned moral lessons by observing other people.

How could he tell? In his own words, babies are about as useful as slugs in terms of behaviour experiments as they don't have the motor skills to do useful things such as pull levers, go through mazes or even pick up an item they prefer. But the preferences of babies can be deduced by what they choose to look at and for how long their gaze rests on something.

Helpful and unhelpful shapes

Using this measure, he let babies watch helpful and unhelpful animated shapes (yes, really) and then worked out which they favoured. A red ball was shown struggling to get up a hill. It was then either helped (nudged upwards) by a kindly square, or hindered (its path blocked) by an unhelpful triangle. Bloom switched the shapes around to avoid interference by any preference for one shape over the other.

The babies showed a very strong preference for the helpful shape. The effect was strengthened if the shapes had faces. Interestingly, the preference disappeared if the babies didn't first see the ball trying to get up the hill – so the social interaction between the shapes was important, not just the physical movement. Babies as young as three months old preferred to look at the helpful shapes.

The good, the bad, and the indifferent

When Bloom introduced a neutral character, a shape that neither helped nor hindered the hill-climbing circle, babies of six months and older preferred the helpful shape to the neutral shape, and the neutral shape to the hindering shape. Babies of three months old didn't distinguish between helping and neutral, but still disliked the hindering shape. This is in keeping with the 'negativity bias' common in adults and children – we have a greater sensitivity to bad stuff than to good stuff, and are more likely to respond to something negative than to something positive. We will complain about someone who does an unkind or outrageous act, but not as many of us will applaud someone who does a kindly act. Bloom concluded that babies can recognize considerate and inconsiderate behaviour very early on in their development – probably before they can be said to have learned it as they won't have been exposed to clear models. He suggests that this indicates an innate moral sense, with the brain primed with a simple sense of morality right from the start.

Play nicely

Karen Wyn, also at Yale, carried out another experiment, this time with one-year-olds. The children watched a puppet show in which two puppets played cooperatively but a third took away the ball they were playing with and ran off. The children were then shown the puppets, with a reward in front of each, and asked to remove the reward from one of them. Most toddlers removed the reward from the 'naughty' puppet. One boy not only removed the reward, but hit

the 'naughty' puppet. This experiment adds the ideas of reward and punishment to recognition of moral actions. At a year old, a child is already developing a sense of justice.

Not all good

Studies with puppets are quite a good way of finding out what babies prefer, but we might not always like what we discover. Wyn's work with helpful and unhelpful puppets also showed that small children were happy when puppets they thought were like them (puppets that 'chose' the same food as the children liked) were helped, but were also happy when puppets unlike them (that chose food the children disliked) were not helped.

Wyn concluded, ominously: 'This reaction seems to suggest the roots of the adult impulses toward xenophobia, prejudice and war.'

DARWIN'S BABY

It's a hard life being the child of a professional biologist. Charles Darwin made detailed observations of and notes on the development of his son, William. He recorded such details as when the boy began to deceive his parents to cover up taking food he wasn't allowed (by hiding the stains on his clothes) – at two years and eight months. The child clearly felt guilt and shame – he had done something that was not allowed, but he had never suffered any punishments, so fear of discovery was not to do with fear of external consequences.

Chapter 8

Wasting your time in a daydream?

Do you spend too much time staring out the window fantasizing? It might be good for you.

If you listened to your teachers at school, you'd get the idea that daydreaming is definitely a waste of time. In fact, the opposite may well be true. Indeed, it may be the wellspring of creativity...

Good or bad?

In the 19th and early 20th centuries, professional opinion generally held that daydreaming is a bad thing. Early psychology textbooks warned that excessive daydreaming could push people towards insanity. An American army recruitment questionnaire in World War I aimed to root out neurotic would-be soldiers by rejecting those who agreed with the statement 'I daydream frequently'. Children who daydream today might find themselves in a 'special needs' class. Yet current estimates put the amount of time we spend daydreaming at 15–50 per cent of our waking hours, so there must be a lot of neurotic people in need of medication if past assessments were correct.

> *'The mind is inherently restless. It's always looking to attend to the most interesting thing in its environment. Oftentimes, the most interesting thing is going on in the internal environment.'*
> Jonathan Schooler, University of California, Santa Barbara

Freud saw daydreams, like night-time dreaming, as revealing repressed thoughts, desires and memories. He also saw them as a type of wish-fulfilment, in which we can have anything we want.

That sounds quite nice. There is more and more evidence that daydreaming is constructive and useful. In the 1980s, psychologist Eric Klinger found that for people with dull, repetitive jobs that don't occupy the mind, or jobs that involve long periods of inactivity (such as being a lifeguard), daydreaming is a way of staving off boredom and frustration, keeping the brain active. Of those he studied, 75 per cent of people with jobs that don't require much concentration said they daydreamed to alleviate boredom.

Klinger gave participants a beeper and told them to write about any daydreams they were having each time it sounded. He discovered that daydreaming frequency varied hugely, with people recording anything from six to 176 daydreams during a day. He found that most

> *'You can engage in trial action without any consequences. You can imagine yourself ridiculing your teachers or beating up your boss without actually doing it.'*
> Psychologist Jerome Singer, 1966

of our daydreaming is not ornate fantasy. Instead most consists of mundane rehearsal and replaying of episodes in everyday life. Counter to Freud's suggestion that daydreaming takes us to places we don't feel allowed to go in normal life, only 5 per cent of Klinger's sample reported daydreams with sexual content, and few had violent daydreams.

Better things to do?

Daydreaming is considered a problem when it prevents someone getting on with the task in hand – for example, when a schoolchild stares out of the window thinking through strategies for a computer game instead of listening to the teacher. But there is evidence that those who daydream a lot are more creative and more empathetic than those who don't. Klinger found that among a group of Israeli students, those who daydreamed were more empathetic than those who didn't.

Being aware of daydreaming is an indicator

> ### HARVEST YOUR DAYDREAMS
>
> If you're not going to pay attention to what you should be doing, you might as well pay attention to what you actually are doing. Harvesting daydreams for ideas is a habit found among many successful and creative people. Einstein conceived the theory of relativity when daydreaming about riding a beam of light. George de Mestral came up with the idea for Velcro when picking burrs from his clothes and his dog's coat after a mountain walk. Many creative people carry a notebook and jot down ideas that come to them from nowhere, knowing they will otherwise forget them. You can use your mobile phone if you don't have a notebook.

of how useful it is to us. In a study conducted by Jonathan Schooler in Santa Barbara, California, students who daydreamed while trying to read a story came up with more creative answers when asked later to think up alternative uses for everyday objects such as a coat-hanger and a toothpick than those who didn't daydream.

Schooler points out that daydreaming doesn't serve the goal in hand, but it can serve longer-term goals.

That's why teachers want to stop a child daydreaming – it might make them more creative and happier in the long run, but the teacher needs to get the child to focus on the short-term goal of learning the lesson.

Default mode network

Marcus E. Raichle at the University of Washington has used an enhanced brain scanning technique called functional MRI (fMRI) to discover which bits of the brain are active when we daydream. He found that parts dealing with sensory input (sights, sounds, smells) and parts involved in building and processing memory are all involved. He dubbed this set of brain functions the 'default network' as it's the activity the brain defaults to when not doing anything else.

Raichle has described it as the 'backbone of consciousness'.

It's been suggested that monitoring the activity of the default network might be useful in medicine, for example, by diagnosing Alzheimer's disease and assessing the effectiveness of treatments, or testing the level of consciousness in coma patients. The brain-dead have no activity in the default network, but those in a deep coma or permanent.

WHAT DO YOU THINK WHEN YOU THINK OF NOTHING?

Most of us, with nothing else to think about, daydream. But people with Asperger's syndrome or autism tend to daydream much less than others. Russell Hurlburt at the University of Nevada studied the 'idle brain' activity of three men with Asperger's and found that they either could not grasp the concept of 'inner life' or reported only images and objects – they did not construct inner narratives.

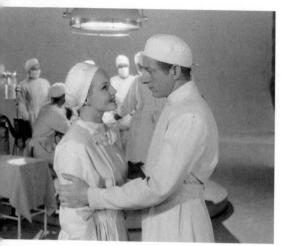

In James Thurber's short story 'The Secret Life of Walter Mitty' (1939) the protagonist is a mild and ineffectual man who has extravagant, fanciful daydreams, as a pilot or surgeon, for example. But most people's daydreams aren't fantasies in which they act heroically. Instead, most of us replay arguments, coming up with smart rejoinders to slights, or plan the evening meal, or imagine what will happen when we take the car to the garage.

vegetative state still show 65 per cent of normal activity. Those in a state of minimal consciousness still show 90 per cent of normal activity. It's possible that measuring activity in the default network might be a way of anticipating which unconscious patients have the best chance of recovery.

Three varieties

Psychologist Jerome Singer has spent six decades on research into daydreams. Singer had a vibrant inner life as a child and took a professional interest in daydreams, wanting to discover how different people daydream and what purpose daydreaming serves.

Singer identified three distinct types of daydreaming:

- **positive constructive daydreaming** engages in playful, vivid and wishful imagery. This is the type that is good for nurturing creativity.
- **guilty-dysphoric daydreaming** involves anxiety or dread and can be distressing. It produces images of heroism, failure, aggression, and ambition. This type includes the obsessive reliving of past trauma associated with post-traumatic stress disorder (PTSD).
- **poor attentional control** is the distracted type of daydreaming, often characterized by anxiety, that plagues us when we try – and fail – to concentrate. It's the noonday demon of old (see page 125).

Daydreaming is good for you

Focusing on 'positive constructive daydreaming', Singer and later Schooler found that daydreaming can serve several broad functions:

- It helps planning, enabling us to envisage and map out future actions. Daydreaming allows us to rehearse future events by visualizing and planning alternative outcomes.
- It helps with problem-solving, and allows creativity to flourish.
- It helps us with 'attentional cycling', letting us switch between

focuses of attention or streams of information and so building a more meaningful and integrated approach towards personal or external goals.

- It provides 'dishabituation' – by breaking up a task or focus we achieve more distributed practice, and that's been found to make for more solid learning. (It's why four half-hour slots of revision before a test are more effective than one unbroken two-hour stint.)

Daydreaming seems to have considerable personal and emotional benefits, helping us to develop compassion, moral reasoning, understanding of the perspectives and emotions of others, and gathering meaning from events and experiences.

Letting off steam

Daydreaming can also provide a safety valve. If we imagine ourselves responding aggressively to a given situation, it can relieve our tension and frustration, leaving us content to provide a more measured response. Only occasionally, for some individuals, imagined aggression translates into real violence. Fantasizing about outcomes or responses can also provide some satisfaction or amelioration of bad feelings if things have gone badly for us. Imagining shouting at your boss or punching your neighbour can make you feel better without you actually having to do it.

Einstein had many of his ideas during his violin breaks, and believed that the best insights came about through 'combinatory play' – the putting together of different ideas. Many people have defined creativity or inspiration as joining ideas or knowledge from different realms in new or unexpected ways. The most creative people are often those who can forge links or see connections between very disparate concepts. Not only do the links spring up during

daydreaming, but the raw material is often garnered during 'idle' activity such as aimlessly surfing the web or skimming magazines.

Good for whom?

Positive, constructive daydreaming, on balance, is good for personal development and satisfaction, but sometimes it might be costly in terms of external goals. That means it's good for your inner self, but not necessarily good for your public self – the 'you' that tutors and employers are relating to. Ultimately, that means you might need to moderate your level of daydreaming, since you still need to get an education or hold down a job.

> 'What is most truly human about man, what is perhaps his greatest gift derived from evolution and perhaps his greatest resource in his mastery of the environment and of himself, is his capacity for fantasy.'
> Psychologist Jerome Singer

Day-nightmares

The bad type of daydreaming is, in extremes, associated with mental distress and psychological illness. The nightmare daydreaming of depression is rumination – the constant picking over of distressing memories or thoughts. Instead of the mind drifting to pleasurable plans for a hot date or useful inventions, it returns again and again to the replaying of past mistakes or slights. Like picking at a scab, it doesn't make the wound any better, but prolongs the agony. A common feature of post-traumatic stress disorder (PTSD) is replaying the traumatic incident, either consciously or in flashbacks. Again, it's not a healthy type of daydreaming. In depressed people, a particular part of the default network becomes very active. The subgenual anterior cingulate cortex, more helpfully known as the 'sadness node', goes into overdrive as people suffering from depression ruminate or relive painful memories.

Chapter 9
Would you do that again?

What makes us do things? Conditioning can forge strange links between stimuli and actions.

Do you get hungry if you look at pictures in a food magazine? Do you feel uncomfortable if you see a video about surgery? Your brain makes connections between the knowledge you have and specific bodily functions and sensations. Responding to some stimuli is instinct – salivating when we see food, for example. Other responses

PAVLOV'S DOGS

Russian physiologist Ivan Pavlov (1849–1936) studied the workings of the digestive system. While conducting experiments with dogs he discovered the conditioned reflex – a learned physical response to a stimulus. Dogs will usually salivate whenever they see food – it is an instinct that prepares the dog to eat. The food is a primary reflex that produces a response – salivating. Pavlov repeatedly made a noise with a buzzer, whistle, bell, tuning fork or other instrument before feeding his experimental dogs. As usual, the dogs salivated when their food arrived. After a while, the dogs began to associate the noise with the imminent arrival of food and began salivating as soon as they heard it – before they had even seen the food. Although salivating is an automatic response that can't be controlled directly, the dogs' brains had set up a connection between the sound and the arrival of food, so this secondary stimulus produced the same response.

are conditioned – if we have had bad experiences at the dentist, our anxiety levels might rise as soon as we walk through the dentist's door.

Conditioned responses can make us fear things that are not, in themselves, scary. Conditioning can also lead us to do things or not do them because of the response they bring. This type of conditioning is used in child rearing and dog training.

A job frightening small children

Whatever you think of experimenting on animals as Pavlov did, few people would now condone the notorious 'Little Albert' experiments.

In 1919, John Watson and

PSYCHOBABBLE: CLASSICAL AND OPERANT CONDITIONING

Classical conditioning is the same as Pavlovian conditioning; the body is taught by repeated exposure to give a response to an unrelated stimulus – such as drooling at the sound of a bell because the bell is known to signal food.

Operant conditioning is strengthening or weakening a spontaneous action by means of rewarding or punishing it.

For example, if a rat finds pressing a lever delivers a drink of sugar water, it will perform the action repeatedly.

The consequences reinforce the behaviour.

If pressing the lever delivers an electric shock, the rat will stop pressing the lever.

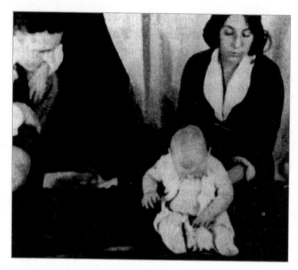

Rosalie Rayner recruited a nine-month-old baby boy from the campus nursery to use in their behaviour experiments. He was known as 'Little Albert' although in 2009 his real name was revealed to be Douglas Merritte. Watson and Rayner began the experiment by exposing 'Little Albert' to a range of harmless objects and animals, including a white laboratory rat. He was not afraid of any of them. Then Watson and Rayner proceeded to frighten 'Albert'. When he touched the rat, they made a loud noise behind him by striking a piece of metal with a hammer. The boy cried. They did this repeatedly until Albert cried whenever he saw the rat. As soon as it appeared, Albert would turn away from it and try to escape from the experimental bench.

The association extended to other furry objects, so that Albert was

THE LAW OF EFFECT

Soon after the publication of Pavlov's experiments on classical conditioning in dogs in Russia, Edward Thorndike began working on operant conditioning with cats in the USA. Thorndike built a 'puzzle box' that a cat could only escape from by pressing a lever or pulling on a loop. He put a hungry cat in the box. It had to free itself before it could get any food. Thorndike noted that it took quite a while for the cat to stumble on the escape mechanism the first time, but with successive box-trips, it took the cat less and less time to escape. Thorndike defined the law of effect: a pleasing after-effect strengthens (encourages) the action that produced it. Modern psychologists would call this 'positive reinforcement' – the good effect of escaping the box reinforces the cat's action in using the lever or loop.

also afraid of a rabbit, a dog, a furry coat and even Watson himself, when he appeared in a Santa Claus mask with a fuzzy beard (which sounds as though it might have been frightening even without the conditioning). The study showed that the kind of classical conditioning Pavlov had managed with dogs was also applicable to humans.

Not so good

There was much that was wrong with Watson and Rayner's experiment, not least that it was unethical and cruel. Albert was not desensitized afterwards, and so presumably remained afraid of rats, rabbits and all other furry animals. He moved away with his parents and there was no opportunity for follow-up studies or therapy. In fact, he died at the age of six from hydrocephalus, which he'd had since birth. Contrary to Watson's claims that he was a normal, healthy baby, Albert did not develop normally (and Watson probably knew this). That made him unsuitable as a subject representing normal development. Further, Watson and Rayner had no system for measuring Albert's responses other than their own subjective judgments.

Better conditions

In 1924, Mary Cover Jones used conditioning more ethically to help a child with a phobia of white, furry things – just what Albert might have benefited from a few years later. The child, Peter, was most afraid of a white rabbit. Over time, the experimenter brought Peter and the rabbit closer together until eventually the boy was able to pet and play with the rabbit without fear. Other children, who were

STAGES OF LOSING FEAR OF RABBITS

Mary Cover Jones reported the following stages of interaction between Peter and the rabbit:

A. Rabbit anywhere in the room in a cage causes fear reactions.
B. Rabbit 12 feet away in cage tolerated.
C. Rabbit 4 feet away in cage tolerated.
D. Rabbit 3 feet away in cage tolerated.
E. Rabbit close in cage tolerated.
F. Rabbit free in room tolerated.
G. Rabbit touched when experimenter holds it.
H. Rabbit touched when free in room.
I. Rabbit defied by spitting at it, throwing things at it, imitating it.
J. Rabbit allowed on tray of high chair.
K. Squats in defenceless position beside rabbit.
L. Helps experimenter to carry rabbit to its cage.
M. Holds rabbit on lap.
N. Stays alone in room with rabbit.
O. Allows rabbit in play pen with him.
P. Fondles rabbit affectionately.
Q. Lets rabbit nibble his fingers.

not afraid of the rabbit, were present in the room, modelling normal responses to the rabbit.

Making things better

The Peter experiment was an early foray into behavioural therapy, which aims to retrain a person's thinking and behaviour. Several types of conditioning are used in therapy, teaching and other kinds of behaviour modification. They can involve punishment or rewards. A punishment is a negative reinforcement – each time the subject does something, a bad thing happens. It aims to reduce an unwanted behaviour. A reward is a positive reinforcement that aims to increase a desired behaviour – giving children a sticker for picking up toys they have dropped, for instance.

Most studies suggest that positive reinforcement is more effective than negative reinforcement (see Chapter 16 – *Carrot or stick?*).

We do it all the time

We use elements of conditioning, and positive and negative reinforcement, all the time without really

5:1

Studies have found that in trying to adjust the behaviour of children a ratio of 5:1, praise:criticism is most effective. According to other studies, the same ratio of praise and criticism works in keeping marriages stable.

Phobias are still treated in the way that Mary Cover Jones dealt with Peter's aversion to white, furry things. Gradually increasing exposure in a safe, controlled environment erodes a person's irrational fears.

thinking. When childcare manuals suggest giving a child a bedtime routine, they are exploiting a form of conditioning.

The child who every day has a warm bath, a story and then goes to sleep will, after a while, start to feel sleepy because the warm bath and story always lead to sleep.

A dog that is taken for a walk when a child comes home from school will get excited on hearing the door open in the afternoon. A child who is praised for cleaning her teeth will, after a while, clean them even when the parent who gives praise is away for a few days.

Chapter 10

Why won't you get up?

Why do teenagers stay in bed half the day?
Are they just lazy?

Anyone with a teenager, or who remembers being a teenager, will know that teens like to stay in bed until well past normal getting-up time. They also like to stay up until well beyond any normal going-to-bed time. Left to their own devices, they'll often stay up until 4am and sleep until the afternoon. Is it just perversity and rebellion? Or is there a good reason for such antisocial timekeeping?

'There's a biological predisposition for going to bed late and getting up late. Clearly you can impose upon that even worse habits, but they are not lazy.'
Russell Foster, Professor of Circadian Neuroscience, Oxford University

Your personal clock

Everyone has an internal clock – or 'body clock' – that regulates the natural cycles of the body. This pattern of daily activities in your body is called the 'circadian rhythm'. Circadian rhythms determine

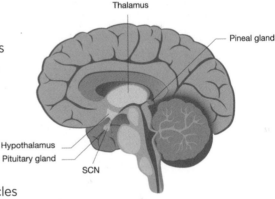

The body clock is located in the hypothalamic suprachiasmatic nucleus (SCN), a tiny group of cells at the base of the brain.

HOW YOU'RE LIKE A MUSHROOM

It's not just human beings that have circadian rhythms. Many – perhaps all – organisms on Earth have 'body clocks' that are attuned to a roughly 24-hour day. Nocturnal animals sleep all day and hunt at night, but they still work to a 24-hour cycle. Even fungi have circadian rhythms and produce spores at a particular time of day. Scientists researching circadian rhythms often work with a fungus called Neurospora crassa. They have found genes that control the relation of activity in the fungus to times of day. Mutation in those genes messes up the fungus's body clock. Presumably it lies around doing nothing all day when its circadian rhythms are disrupted. Oh, wait...

such things as when you are most active, when you feel tired and so on. Most of us are not able to work entirely in synch with our circadian rhythms as we are bound by convention and financial need to go to work at hours of our employers' choosing, get our children up and off to school, feed hungry babies or be awake for deliveries and appointments. Throw in a seven-hour stint on Fatal Fantasy 9 overnight and the day's not looking too good.

Night owls and larks

We're used to the idea that some people function best – are most alert and amenable to work – in the evenings and for others the best time is in the mornings. This distinction between 'evening people' and 'morning people' is commonly acknowledged with

> *'Every time you come in yelling that God damn "Rise and Shine!" "Rise and Shine!" I say to myself, "How lucky dead people are!"'*
> Tennessee Williams,
> *The Glass Menagerie*

the labels 'night owls' and 'larks'. If you like to stay up late and get up late, you're a night owl. If you like to go to bed early and get up early, you're a lark. There's nothing wrong with either, but if you're

HOW LONG IS A DAY?

A day is not exactly 24 hours long. There are different ways of measuring and defining a day, but it is normally held to be just over 23 hours and 56 minutes. The Earth is gradually slowing in its orbit, so a day is steadily getting longer by about 1.7 milliseconds per century. It doesn't sound much, but it adds up. Around 620 million years ago, when organisms more interesting than slime were just getting going, the day was only 21.9 hours long. Dinosaurs, however, would have had circadian rhythms close to ours, with a day of around 23 hours and 40 minutes.

Hallucigenia (c. 640 mya) would have worked to a day of around 21 hours long. It had to wait more days between birthdays, too.

a lark you'll struggle with partying until 4am and if you're a night owl you won't like a job that involves a commute starting at 6am.

Night owls and larks are at opposite ends of the normal spectrum for circadian rhythms. Night owls might need a loud alarm to get

them up in the morning, but they will get up. They are not generally dysfunctional.

Jet lag

Whether you're a night owl or a lark, if you've taken a long flight that crosses several time zones, you are likely to have experienced jet lag. It occurs when your circadian rhythms have been severely disrupted

CAN YOU AVOID JET LAG?

The chemical melatonin is a hormone produced in the pineal gland, deep in the brain. It plays an important role in regulating circadian rhythms. Melatonin is produced when it gets dark, and helps to regulate the body's temperature during sleep. Trials have found that taking melatonin by mouth at bedtime after a flight reduces jet lag in nine out of ten people. Jet lag is worst, and melatonin most effective, when flying east and crossing four or more time zones.

Combining sleeping tablets to get to sleep and coffee to stay awake is not an effective treatment for jet lag. Sleeping on the plane doesn't reduce jet lag unless it's at a time you would normally sleep. Neither of these approaches readjusts the body's internal clock. Dehydration makes jet lag worse, so drinking alcohol to forget won't work.

If you're only travelling for a couple of days, it's not worth trying to reset your body clock on the trip. Otherwise, stay in the dark for at least three hours after arriving if you're flying east. If you're flying west, get into daylight when you arrive.

– for example, by being expected to sleep when your body thinks it's the middle of the day, or to attend meetings when your body thinks it's after midnight.

Over a few days, exposure to your current pattern of night and day nudges your body clock into synch with the local time zone and you feel better.

The teenage body clock

Mary Carskadon, Professor of Human Behavior at Brown University, USA, has carried out extensive research into the circadian rhythms of children and adolescents. Her findings bear out what any teenager will tell you – they really *can't* get up at 7am and function normally.

At puberty, the brain undergoes many changes, including changes to the biological body clock. This equips them for teenage life, enabling them to stay up late at parties and gigs and to sleep through any number of alarm clocks and shouting parents until mid-day or later. Unfortunately, as Carskadon points out, it doesn't equip them for school or college starting at 8–8.30am.

Carskadon has shown that even if teenagers

Using technology that emits light, especially for games that raise arousal levels, filling the body with adrenaline, makes sleep elusive. Teenagers make this disconnect from normal working hours even worse by using computers and smart phones late into the night.

go to bed early they don't actually get to sleep then. Getting up early for school means they are sleep-deprived during the week and desperate to catch up with sleep at the weekend – hence staying in bed until the afternoon. Teens need 9¼ hours' sleep, and generally can't get to sleep before 11pm – it's simply not possible to have the sleep they need and get to school on time. Her studies show that the mismatch between the school day and the biological needs of adolescents has many effects, including poor performance at studies and underachievement. Carskadon believes that the school day should be changed to accommodate the different biological rhythms of teens, but the disruption that would cause for everyone else means that it is unlikely to happen.

Sleeping sickness?

Too little sleep can also lead to psychiatric disorders including depression. Psychologist Jane Ansell found that around 50 per cent of teenagers in Scotland are sleep-deprived. Some have been misdiagnosed with attention deficit hyperactivity disorder (ADHD) and other psychological problems – when all they needed is more sleep.

Social jet lag

Some teenagers have an even rougher deal and suffer from a more severe form of this disjunction between normal life and body clock,

DIAGRAM OF THE BIOLOGICAL CLOCK

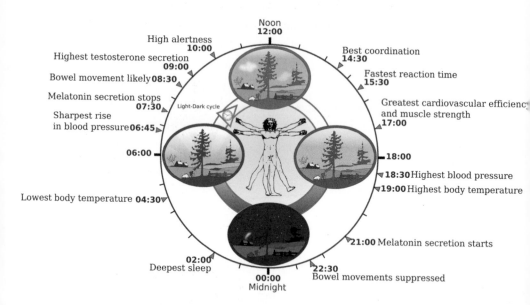

Noon
12:00

High alertness
10:00

Highest testosterone secretion
09:00

Bowel movement likely **08:30**

Melatonin secretion stops
07:30

Sharpest rise
in blood pressure **06:45**

Light-Dark cycle

06:00

Lowest body temperature **04:30**

Best coordination
14:30

Fastest reaction time
15:30

Greatest cardiovascular efficiency
and muscle strength
17:00

18:00

18:30 Highest blood pressure

19:00 Highest body temperature

21:00 Melatonin secretion starts

22:30
Bowel movements suppressed

02:00
Deepest sleep

00:00
Midnight

called delayed sleep phase disorder (DSPD). If this condition starts in
adolescence, it usually disappears at the end of adolescence, but if it
starts in early childhood, it's generally a life-long disorder. This affects
0.15 per cent of adults.

For sufferers, it is like permanent jet lag and so has been called
'social jet lag'. It can sometimes be corrected with medication

or careful, extended therapy with daylight lamps and structured changes to sleeping times. Many people with DSPD are dubbed lazy, antisocial or lacking in willpower – and not just as teenagers. Some cope by taking jobs that require working nights.

ALT-SHIFT-DELETE?

In shift workers, the body clock gets messed around endlessly, and this can do serious harm. A study published in 2014 found that working a night shift disrupted the activity of those genes that normally display varying levels of activity during the day. This applies to nearly 6 per cent of our genes. They are not evenly disturbed, so different parts of the body end up working to different clocks. One of the researchers likened it to having clocks in each room in a house that are set to different times. The lasting effects could include physical as well as psychological harm, such as obesity, diabetes and heart disease.

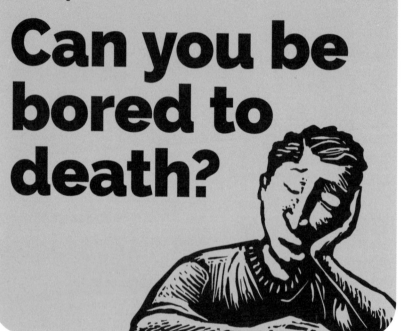

Chapter 11

Can you be bored to death?

Being bored is more interesting and varied than you might imagine.

If you have children, you'll be familiar with the pained cry 'I'm bored' in the holidays. Does boredom serve a purpose? Why do we get bored?

> *'Boredom is not an end product; it is, comparatively, rather an early stage in life and art. You've got to go by or past or through boredom, as through a filter, before the clear product emerges.'*
> F. Scott Fitzgerald

This boring cave...

In prehistory, did cavemen (and cavewomen) get bored? Is that why they painted on the walls? If so, it was the women who were most bored, as research into comparative finger and palm sizes shows that most cave paintings were created by women. And when they had had enough of painting recognizable things, they seem to have played a game that involved jumping as high as they could, as shown by groups of circles made with fingertips on the roofs of some caves.

If there's nothing to do in the cave you might as well paint some animals and then paint around your hands...

The noonday demon

Boredom with doing something dull is not the same

as boredom with not doing anything.

Many people have genuinely boring jobs – they take objects off shelves and put them into trolleys to fulfil orders in a warehouse or supermarket. They clean the floors of empty buildings. They do tasks that are not fulfilling, that don't involve engagement with other people, and that need to be done over and over again. It's easy to see how such tasks could be boring.

> *'The mind is constantly whirling from psalm to psalm... tossed about fickle and aimless through the whole body of Scripture.'*
> St John Cassian, c.360–435

Other people have jobs that shouldn't be boring, but still they can't settle to them. We stare at the computer screen, or out of the window, fiddle with our phones, flick to a social network site, even if our work is something that interests us in principle. It's not a new problem. The mind-wandering was known to medieval monks as 'acedia' ('ἀκηδία') and called the noonday demon (a name since appropriated for depression). It was familiar to the Desert Fathers, those early Christian ascetics who spent their time in contemplation, philosophizing and study. This is not boredom of the same kind. It's being amenable to distractions even though we have something to do that should be challenging and engaging.

These early writers recognized the problem of trying to stay focused on intellectual activity in solitude. St Cassian writes of Paul, living in the desert but provided with all he needed, spending his days making things from date palms and then, at the end of the year, burning them all because:

'...without working with his hands a monk cannot endure to abide in his place, nor can he climb any nearer the summit of holiness: and

'*The demon of acedia – also called the noonday demon – is the one that causes the most serious trouble of all. He presses his attack upon the monk about the fourth hour and besieges the soul until the eighth hour. First of all he makes it seem that the sun barely moves, if at all, and that the day is fifty hours long. Then he constrains the monk to look constantly out the windows, to walk outside the cell, to gaze carefully at the sun to determine how far it stands from the ninth hour, to look now this way and now that to see if perhaps [one of the brethren appears from his cell]. ... This demon drives him along to desire other sites where he can more easily procure life's necessities, more readily find work and make a real success of himself...*'
Evagrius the Solitary, AD345–399

though necessity of making a livelihood in no way demands it, let it be done for the sole purging of the heart, the steadying of thought, perseverance in the cell, and the conquest and final overthrow of accidie itself.'

This recalls the adage 'the devil makes work for idle hands'. The monk who has nothing he must do, must yet do something as to do nothing is dangerous. The suggestion, too, is that it is intellectual work that makes us especially prone to this type of mind-wandering or ennui. The monk must work with his hands. If he does that, he will be able to tolerate the work of thinking.

> *'My soul is impatient with itself, as with a bothersome child; its restlessness keeps growing and is forever the same. Everything interests me, but nothing holds me. I attend to everything, dreaming all the while.'*
> Fernando Pessoa, 1888–1935, poet and writer

Hands and brains

Modern neuroscience suggests another possibility, more practical than demons with a brief to distract the holy. A study on rats reveals that lack of physical activity actually changes the shape of brain cells.

Researchers at Wayne State University School of Medicine, in Detroit, Michigan, divided twelve rats into two groups. One group was put into cages with a running wheel and were soon running five kilometres a day. The other group was put into cages with no wheels and so had a sedentary lifestyle. After three months, the inactive rats had grown extra branches on the neurons in part of their brains. This made them extra-sensitive to stimuli and prone to send extra nerve signals around the brain. The researchers were interested in the implications for heart disease, but it seems that a 'jumpy brain' from inactivity might be more than just a simple proneness to distraction but a genuine neurological phenomenon.

'She only said, "My life is dreary"...' W. E. F. Britten's sketch of Tennyson's bored heroine, Mariana.

Sick of doing nothing

Being bored because you have nothing to do is rather different from failure to engage fully or pay attention to the task in hand. Boredom from doing nothing comes in two categories, giving a total of three types of boredom: bored by a dull task, acedia, and bored with doing nothing. It's possible to be bored because there is too much choice of activity.

For example, the child bored in the holidays might have many options – riding a bike, playing with numerous toys or friends, reading, doing chores (God forbid) – but none of them appeals.

This, like being bored while doing a task, is a failure of attention. None of the possible activities holds the child's attention. Yet the bored prisoner is prevented from doing anything at all.

> **TOO MUCH CHOICE**
> Too much choice can be as bad as having too little. For example, if a restaurant has just three or four set menus, it's easy to choose one of them. But if a restaurant has pages and pages of different options, you will find it much harder to make up your mind.

Many parents have discovered that the best way to get a child to eat is to offer only two options. Even if they don't really want either, they'll know the one they have is better than the alternative, whereas too wide a choice leaves them thinking something else might have been better.

Bored to death

The phrase 'bored to death' was first used by Charles Dickens in *Bleak House*. Indeed, the novel provided the first use of the word 'bored' in that sense.

We commonly think of boredom as something rather trivial, but it has been associated with depression and anxiety disorders. Boredom – having nothing to do – has also been blamed for criminal and antisocial behaviour and implicated in risky behaviours such as drug-taking and compulsive gambling, with people seeking thrills to escape the boredom of their lives.

'And I am bored to death with it. Bored to death with this place, bored to death with my life, bored to death with myself.'
Lady Deadlock, in *Bleak House*, by Charles Dickens, 1852–53

The distress boredom causes is acknowledged in its use as a punishment in prisons the world over. It's important, though, to get the balance right. Boredom is a matter of life and death in more ways than one. If prisoners are too bored, it can be fatal. One of two prisoners convicted of killing another inmate in Long Larton prison, England, when asked why he had killed the man, said, 'I'm bored, it was something to do.' It's an excuse echoed by many a 'bored' teenager who has written on walls, kicked down bus shelters and even beaten up elderly people.

The 17th-century philosopher and mathematician Blaise Pascal thought boredom more than trivial. He saw it as a kind of terrible existential angst that could only be dealt with by filling life with purpose – and, this being 17th-century France, that purpose was God: **'We seek rest in a struggle against some obstacles. And when we have overcome these, rest proves unbearable because of the boredom it produces... only an infinite and immutable object – that is, God himself – can fill this infinite abyss.'**
Pensées, published posthumously (Pascal died in 1662)

Later, both Martin Heidegger (1889–1976) and Arthur Schopenhauer (1788–1860) picked up this theme, with a predictably gloomy outcome. Schopenhauer maintained that if life had any real value, we would never be bored because life itself would suffice. Heidegger concurs, though with not quite so damning a verdict on life:

'Profound boredom, drifting here and there in the abysses of our existence like a muffling fog, removes all things and men and oneself along with it into a remarkable indifference.

This boredom reveals being as a whole.'
Martin Heidegger, 1929

So – what should you do with that bored child?

First, let them be bored for a bit! Being bored is useful; boredom is
the mother of many a creative project (see F. Scott Fitzgerald, page
125). Children need to learn to occupy themselves and to manage
their time – it's a vital life-skill. They need to work out what interests
them and what doesn't;
they can't do that if they
are fed a constant stream of
amusements. The only thing
psychologists think you really
shouldn't do is dump your
bored children in front of a TV
or computer screen. Screen-
based activities produce
little doses of dopamine in
the brain, a chemical that
contributes to learning and
concentration. It's easy
for children to become
accustomed to the higher

level of dopamine that screen activities produce, and then find it harder to concentrate on activities that don't deliver the higher dopamine hit. Children who use screens too much of the time can find it harder to concentrate when doing non-screen activities. If you want to wean them off screen-time later, you'll have a harder job on your hands than helping them find something to do now.

Of course, the same goes for you. If you're bored, a computer game, social networking session or a box-set of DVDs will keep you happy this time, but might make you even more prone to being bored later.

SCREENS OR SCREAMS?

It's the easiest thing in the world to plonk a toddler in front of a TV screen or give them a table computer to play with. But the American Academy of Pediatrics recommends you don't. Their recommended screen-times for children are:

- Up to 2 years old: none
- Ages 3–6 years old: 4–6 hours per week, with the activities discussed and chosen carefully
- Ages 6–14: 6–8 hours a week (good luck with that! A survey in 2010 found young people aged 8–18 spend an average of 7½ hours a day on electronic media)
- Ages 14–18: let them set their own limits, in discussion with you. They need to learn to be self-regulating.

Chapter 12
How cruel can you be?

You might think you would never harm someone
who hasn't harmed you. But can you be sure?

Would you deliver electric shocks to another person, innocent of any crime, just because someone told you to? No? Are you sure? We are far more susceptible to authority than we might like to think.

> *'When you think of the long and gloomy history of man, you will find more hideous crimes have been committed in the name of obedience than have ever been committed in the name of rebellion.'*
> C.P. Snow, 1961

The incredulity with which Ron Jones' students met his account of Nazi Germany is a common response (see page 54). Most normal people find it hard to believe that ordinary German citizens, just like any one of us, could be persuaded to torture and execute their fellow humans. Were the Germans who became Nazis somehow different?

The Milgram experiment

Stanley Milgram, a psychologist at Yale University, Connecticut, was interested in the defence given by many ex-Nazis that they had just been following orders. He was curious to discover how far ordinary people would follow orders. So he decided to find out.

In 1961, Milgram recruited forty volunteers to help with a study of learning, all of them men between the ages of twenty and fifty (and thus comparable to those who might have become SS guards in Nazi Germany). He told them they would be randomly allocated roles as learners or teachers, but in fact all volunteers were to be teachers and all the 'learners' were confederates of Milgram's – actors briefed to play their part. The teachers were instructed to ask questions of a learner in an adjacent room. They were told the learner would be strapped to a chair with two electrodes attached to his body. If the learner got a question wrong, the volunteer (the teacher) was required to administer an electric shock. The volunteer was told that shocks were painful but not harmful. The shocks were mild to start with, but seemingly became more extreme as the learner gave more wrong answers, increasing progressively (they were told) from 15 volts to 450 volts – a dangerous level of shock.

> '*Could it be that Eichmann and his million accomplices in the Holocaust were just following orders? Could we call them all accomplices?*'
> Stanley Milgram, 1974

Scripted torture

The actors could be heard screaming, struggling in their chairs and begging to be released as they were apparently subjected to more

experimenter

teacher

learner

and more pain. At 300 volts, following a script, the learner banged on the wall, begging to be let out. Above that level of shock the learner was silent, giving no more responses. The volunteer was told to consider silence to be a wrong answer and continue increasing the shocks. The experimenter sat in the room with the volunteer and, if the volunteer balked at the idea of administering a shock, encouraged him by using the following scripted prompts, in order:

1. Please continue.
2. The experiment requires you to continue.
3. It is absolutely essential that you continue.
4. You have no other choice but to continue.

You can find audio files and videos of the experiment online.

Just say yes

The results Milgram reported were alarming. All volunteers continued to administer shocks up to 300 volts and nearly two-thirds (65 per cent) of volunteers continued all the way to the highest level of shock, 450 volts. Milgram concluded that we have an overwhelming urge to obey an authority figure – even one as seemingly powerless as a scientific researcher.

Milgram debriefed his volunteers, explaining the experiment to them and noted down how they reacted. He identified three types of volunteer by their responses:

- Obeyed, but justified themselves – they shifted responsibility on to the experimenter or, in some cases, the learner (for being stupid).
- Obeyed, but blamed themselves – they felt bad about what they had done. Milgram felt this group might act differently if they found themselves in a similar situation in future.
- Rebelled – refused to continue with the experiment, citing the primacy of the learner's wellbeing over the needs of the experiment.

The circumstances of obedience

Milgram repeated his experiment, varying some aspects of the setting to see which factors affected levels of obedience. He found that obedience levels

> *'I set up a simple experiment at Yale University to test how much pain an ordinary citizen would inflict on another person simply because he was ordered to by an experimental scientist. Stark authority was pitted against the subjects' [participants'] strongest moral imperatives against hurting others, and, with the subjects' [participants'] ears ringing with the screams of the victims, authority won more often than not. The extreme willingness of adults to go to almost any lengths on the command of an authority constitutes the chief finding of the study and the fact most urgently demanding explanation.'*
>
> Stanley Milgram, 1974

were higher in the hallowed environment of Yale University, but lower in a run-down office in the city. Levels were higher when the experimenter wore a lab coat and lower when he wore ordinary clothes. People were more obedient when the authority figure (the experimenter) was in the room rather than giving instructions by telephone. Finally, obedience rose considerably when people did not have to press the switch themselves to administer the shock, but delegated the task to an assistant.

Milgram's agency theory

To account for the alacrity with which ordinary people would behave in appalling ways, Milgram proposed his 'agency theory'.

He suggested that we have two different states: autonomous and 'agentic'. In the autonomous state, people make their own choices and take responsibility for their actions. They are governed by their own sets of values and standards. In the agentic state, they act as agents, carrying out orders and feeling they bear no responsibility for their actions as they have not personally sanctioned them.

When faced with a figure of authority, Milgram claimed, most people undergo an 'agentic shift' from the autonomous to the obedient state. This explains why US soldiers obeyed orders to kill unarmed Vietnamese civilians in the village of My Lai in 1968, why Serbian soldiers in Bosnia raped women as an act of war, and accounts for any number of other atrocities committed against the innocent in Rwanda, the Baltic States and Iraq over the last twenty years. Critics complain that no mechanism for this shift has been demonstrated and it's hard to see how it could be measured (if, indeed, it even exists).

> *'Ordinary people, simply doing their jobs, and without any particular hostility on their part, can become agents in a terrible destructive process. Moreover, even when the destructive effects of their work become patently clear, and they are asked to carry out actions incompatible with fundamental standards of morality, relatively few people have the resources needed to resist authority.'*
> Stanley Milgram, 1974

FROM THE HORSE'S MOUTH

At his trial in Jerusalem in 1960, Nazi war criminal Adolf Eichmann referred repeatedly to his role as one of impotent obedience, even though he had been largely in charge of organizing the Holocaust. He described himself as 'one of the many horses pulling the wagon and couldn't escape left or right because of the will of the driver'.

'From my childhood, obedience was something I could not get out of my system. When I entered the armed services at the age of 27, I found being obedient not a bit more difficult than it had been during my life to that point. It was unthinkable that I would not follow orders.

'I personally had nothing to do with this. My job was to observe and report on it.

'Obeying an order was the most important thing to me. It could be that is in the nature of the German.

'Now that I look back, I realize that a life predicated on being obedient and taking orders is a very comfortable life indeed. Living in such a way reduces to a minimum one's own need to think.'

Adolf Eichmann, 1960

Was it true?

Milgram's methodology has been criticized, as well as the ethics of leading the volunteers to believe that they were harming someone. (Several volunteers clearly suffered extreme distress during the experiment. However, they were debriefed afterwards, and Milgram followed up a year later to check that none suffered long-term harm.)

In 2013, psychologist Gina Perry published the findings of her research into the Milgram archive: Milgram's presentation of his results was somewhat selective, conflating all the studies to give a 65 per cent obedience rating. Some volunteers had suspected the deception, while some had surreptitiously 'inflicted' shocks of a lower voltage (but still the intensity of the screams increased). Some asked to check up on the learner or to swap places with him (requests that were refused), and the experimenter had frequently strayed from the script to bully or coerce the volunteer into complying. Further, Milgram's sample was a self-selected group of American males – can it be considered representative of people in general? Whether or not the results of Milgram's study are reliable or statistically accurate, it's clear a significant proportion of people will take obedience far enough to be willing to inflict serious harm on others. Maybe there isn't an inner-Nazi in all of us, but there is an alarming tendency to do as we are told, even if we doubt the morality or wisdom of the order.

Chapter 13

Why are you wasting my time?

Wasting someone's time is unforgivable. So you have to persuade them it wasn't wasted.

We don't like wasting time. We know that time is a valuable commodity and we get frustrated if we are forced to waste it. Never mind that most of us waste a lot of time anyway – it's different if you've chosen to watch junk TV or stare out of the window. What we really don't like is to be forced to wait, when it's obvious we are doing nothing.

Queue quietly

Unlikely as it may seem, there are people who specialize in queue management – in making people behave nicely in queues and feel

THE TOO-EFFICIENT AIRPORT

Houston airport was receiving a large number of complaints from passengers about the length of time they had to wait to reclaim their baggage. The airport responded by employing more luggage handlers so that bags were delivered more quickly. The average wait was cut to eight minutes – but the level of complaints stayed the same.

The airport's next solution was a stroke of genius. They moved the baggage reclaim area much further away from the arrival gates. Now passengers had to walk a lot further – and so use up most of the waiting time – before they got anywhere near the carousels. Instead of waiting for eight minutes, they walked for six and waited for two. Complaints stopped. People no longer felt that they were wasting their time.

that they have had as good an experience as they could have done. If people feel ignored, they are more likely to be grouchy.

They make trouble, or spend less money, or choose not to return. Investing a little in queue management pays dividends.

Organizations that sell services involving a lot of waiting or queuing take advantage of psychological research into queuing and waiting behaviour. If customers can be persuaded to be happy about the queue, they are much less likely to complain about their treatment and far more likely to return.

People's willingness to queue is in direct relation to what they think they are getting. People won't queue long to buy a few items, especially if they have to stand behind people with a lot of shopping who will be getting more for their time – not just more shopping, but more of the sales assistant's attention – than they are.

Walt Disney employs seventy-five industrial engineers around the world to help with queue management in its theme parks.

How long do I have to wait?

People typically overestimate how long they have to wait. If asked how long they have queued for, they claim to have waited, on average, 36 per cent longer than they actually have.

Queue rage is a phenomenon every bit as real as road rage, but it can be reduced if people in the queue are kept informed. If they know how long they will have to wait, they are less likely to get cross – unless the wait is longer than they were led to expect. Some theme parks advertise slightly exaggerated waiting times for the rides because then people are pleasantly surprised rather

than disappointed. They come away feeling that they didn't have to wait too long, and that they have somehow beaten the system. For example, in the ordinary course of events people might grumble about having to wait for thirty minutes. But if they had actually expected to wait forty minutes they are less likely to complain because they now feel they are 'up' by ten minutes.

You aren't doing nothing

Another way of keeping people calm is to give them something to do, such as watching adverts or news updates on a screen. Screens have popped up everywhere

> '*Often the psychology of queuing is more important than the statistics of the wait itself.*'
> Richard Larson, Massachusetts Institute of Technology (MIT)

we have to sit or stand and do nothing. You can watch the news on a bus, on the train, at the post office and in hospital waiting rooms.

Or we might be rewarded (or bribed) with the free sweets in hotel reception areas or free coffee in a clinic or hair salon. The sweets or coffee are scant payment for your precious time, but people don't think of it that way. The value of your time is acknowledged and you are offered something in return for it – never mind that what you are offered is virtually worthless, your subliminal need to be valued is satisfied.

Don't worry

One of the reasons people don't like waiting is that it makes them anxious. They are worried about the time they are losing, and sometimes about what is coming after the wait (at the dentist, for example). If the wait is too long, they might also worry that they have been forgotten.

Speaking to someone or being moved to a different area helps people feel less anxious as they believe they are now being 'seen to' or 'dealt with' – they have begun the process. Waiting as part of a process annoys people less than waiting for a process to begin. So although it makes no difference to how long you have to wait to see a doctor, if you are moved from one waiting area to another after fifteen minutes, it feels less frustrating.

If a nurse takes a quick history of your problem or asks you to fill in a questionnaire, you will feel even better as it seems you are no longer wasting time – even if the nurse does nothing with the information you provide.

Being able to see how many people are waiting ahead of you doesn't really tell you how long you have to wait, but as the numbers tick off you can see progress.

When waiting is sold to you

Have you ever walked past an Apple store the day a new iPad or iPhone is released? The queue often goes round the block – and yet no one minds. The same was true of people queuing at midnight for the latest Harry Potter novel. It's not the same as queuing for the sales or tickets to a popular concert or festival – there's a limited supply of those and only one chance to buy. No one really believes Apple won't make as many iPhones as it can sell, they just won't all be available on the first day.

The illusion of exclusivity is created by a high price point – and queuing. People will spend lots of time in a queue to have a new phone a couple of days before other people. They will even boast about how long they have been queuing, and bond with other people in the queue.

Agency and its lack

One of the reasons we don't like to queue is that we feel we have no control over the situation. In the language of psychology, this 'lack of agency' makes us feel bad. Agency is the sense that we are acting as independent agents, that our fate is in our own hands. It is a combination of empowerment and self-determination.

Lack of agency on a large scale is very damaging to people, leading to frustration, anger and even depression. When asked to give an account of their personal history and circumstances, people with depression frequently locate the source of problems outside themselves. They talk of things happening to them, and of what others have done that has had an impact on them. People who are not depressed tend to put themselves at the centre of their own narrative, saying what they have done, or how they have responded to outside events. They don't represent external events as the driving force of their lives.

Bread, circuses and talent shows

People can be distracted from their lack of agency, and many political systems have attempted to do this (often successfully). When people feel disempowered, they will seize on any apparently power-bestowing situation or

'Already long ago, from when we sold our vote to no man, the People have abdicated our duties; for the People who once upon a time handed out military command, high civil office, legions — everything, now restrains itself and anxiously hopes for just two things: bread and circuses.'
Juvenal, *Satires* (10)

anything that apparently validates their worth.

People today are buffeted by economic and political forces beyond their control, and so feel powerless. In response, they adopt small acts of agency, or *faux*-agency, by voting on talent contests and reality shows and 'making their voice heard' on social networking and news site comment feeds. Did you vote for the talent show winner?

You made that happen. Did you tweet your disgust at a news story? You are part of 'the conversation'.

BUTTONS THAT DO NOTHING

You know those buttons at traffic junctions that look as if they change the lights in your favour? Usually they do nothing of the sort. The lights are on a fixed sequence and the button has no effect on them whatsoever. These buttons that do nothing – called 'placebo buttons', from the Latin placebo, 'I please' – are all over the place. The 'Close Doors' button in a lift often does nothing either. But they give us a sense of agency and make the wait for the lights to change or the lift to arrive feel less of a surrender.

Chapter 14

Why didn't anybody help?

Failing to help someone in trouble isn't just callousness. It's more complicated than that.

Have you ever seen something bad happen, and noticed that other people walked past without helping? Perhaps you also walked past without helping. Sometimes we can tell ourselves we don't want to get involved. If it's a domestic dispute, we can say it's none of our business. If it's a dangerous situation, we can say we don't want to get hurt. But what if someone has had an accident, or collapsed, or is having a fit? People still walk past when there is no risk of danger, or of intruding in an unwelcome way. It's called 'bystander apathy'.

THE MURDER OF KITTY GENOVESE

Kitty Genovese was an Italian-American woman who was attacked and murdered in New York in 1964. Her attacker, Winston Moseley, was still in prison for the murder at the time of writing, some fifty years later. At the time of her murder, newspapers reported that thirty-eight people witnessed or heard the attack but none came to Kitty's aid. Later accounts disputed that so many people were aware of the attack, however, or that no one helped. Whatever the actual events, the case sparked a far-reaching psychological study into this 'bystander apathy' – sometimes now referred to as 'Genovese syndrome'.

And it doesn't just apply to helping others – it can even extend to protecting ourselves.

Who will help?

While intervening in a murder would probably be dangerous, getting help for someone having an epileptic fit would seem an obvious and humane thing to do. Yet, surprisingly, few people actually do go to their aid.

In 1968, prompted by the Genovese case, John Darley and Bibb Latané set up an experiment at Columbia University to discover whether people would help a stranger in distress. They actually asked for volunteers to take part in a psychological study about personal problems. As usual with psychology experiments, that story was just a cover. Because the issues discussed were private, all the discussion was to take place over intercom systems. It was important that the participants couldn't see each other. There were one, four or no other participants in each study.

Partway through a discussion, one participant (really a confederate of the researchers) would fake a seizure. They stuttered, asked for help, said they were ill, became increasingly distressed and said they felt they would die. Other participants could hear this – and each other – over the intercom. They had been told at the start that it was important that all participants remained anonymous – rushing to

> *"I-er-um-I think I-I need-er-if-if could-er-er-somebody er-er-er-er-er-er-er give me a little-er-give me a little help here because-er-I-er-I'm-er-erh-h-having a-a-a real problem-er-right now and I-er-if somebody could help me out it would-it would-er-er s-s-sure be-sure be good . . . because-there-er-er-a cause I-er-I-uh-I've got a-a one of the-er-sei er-er-things coming on and-and-and I could really-er-use some help so if somebody would-er-give me a little h-help-uh-er-er-er-er-er c-could somebody-er-er-help-er-uh-uh-uh (choking sounds). . . . I'm gonna die-er-er-I'm . . . gonna die-er-help-er-er-seizure-er-[chokes, then quiet]."*
>
> Seizure script, Darley and Latané, 1968

someone's aid would compromise that anonymity.

Darley and Latané found that the more people were involved in the discussion, the less likely anyone was to help. Even though they could not see the other participants, they knew they were there. It seemed that each person felt they had less responsibility towards the stranger in distress because there were other people around who should take responsibility. Individual background and gender made no difference to whether people helped. When a participant was the only person involved, they sought help 85 per cent of the time. This dropped to 31 per cent when several other people were involved in the discussion.

Not uncaring

The people who did not seek help were not unfeeling towards the sufferer. They showed symptoms of worry and distress, including sweating and trembling. They appeared to be caught between fear of embarrassment or of spoiling the experiment and distress at the fate of the person having a seizure. When there were no extra participants, the person was much more likely to act. When there

UNCARING

In 2011, a two-year-old girl was run down by a truck in the Chinese city of Foshan. The girl, Yue Yue, lay in the road for seven minutes, and was run over again, while people walked and cycled past her until finally a woman moved her to the side of the road. She later died of her injuries in hospital.

The ensuing global outrage focused on changes in China's social patterns. The possibility of being liable for the girl's medical bills might have been a contributing factor in people's reluctance to help. Guangdong province discussed introducing a law to make it illegal to ignore someone in distress. But it's not about being Chinese. In 2009, twenty people witnessed the rape and murder of a fifteen-year-old girl in Richmond, California. No one called for help, or intervened. Some people even filmed it on their phones. Some bystanders later said they thought it was a joke, people messing about. But no one checked; no one asked if she needed help.

were others, they clearly hoped someone else would do what was needed. Indeed, they relied upon someone else doing it.

How bullies get away with it

If people won't get involved to stop a rape or a murder, or even help an injured toddler, is it surprising bullies can get away with tormenting their targets? Whether in the workplace or the playground, people turn a blind eye to bullying as to other distress. And the more people know about it, the more each one sees it as 'not my problem' and leaves it for someone else to sort out.

We know nothing

One reason for not intervening is what psychologists call 'pluralistic ignorance'. If other people are around, we look to see what their reaction is. If they are not responding as though there is an emergency, or as though someone needs help, we assume that we have misinterpreted the situation. We don't want to look foolish, so we go with the majority position. But if everyone is doing this, and no one actually knows what is going on, the sufferer goes unaided. It's why people drown on a busy beach. People aren't uncaring – they just don't recognize the situation as an emergency.

What's that smoke?

Darley and Latané carried out another experiment with bystanders, but this time it was the participants themselves who seemed to be in danger. They set students to complete questionnaires in a room. After a while, smoke started to leak into the room. The smoke got thicker and thicker until the students could hardly see. Where students were alone in a room filling with smoke, 75 per cent of them would find a way of reporting the problem.

But if they were in a room with two other people who ignored the smoke only 10 per cent raised the alarm. They would rather risk dying of smoke inhalation or burning than embarrassing themselves by raising a false alarm!

Chapter 15
Are you the best 'you' that you can be?

Who are you? Who do you want to be?
Are they the same?

The search for personal fulfilment stretches back millennia. Throughout history, philosophers and religious leaders have suggested how people might improve themselves and their lives. Now psychologists have joined in, and a whole self-help book industry has flourished in the compost of our dissatisfaction. How can you make the most of yourself and your time here?

What is self-actualization?

The goal might be called enlightenment or salvation, personal fulfilment or – most recently – self-actualization, but in any guise it is about living your life well, with meaning and integrity. Whereas religions often impose a preconceived notion of 'living well', self-actualization is about fulfilling your potential, becoming the person you feel you should be, or most want to be – the best ideal 'you'. It's different for everyone, an individual quest with no single script.

> '*What a man can be, he must be. This need we may call self-actualization... It refers to the desire for self-fulfilment, namely, to the tendency for him to become actualized in what he is potentially. This tendency might be phrased as the desire to become more and more what one is, to become everything that one is capable of becoming.*'
>
> Abraham Maslow

ACTUALIZATION

Maslow saw self-actualization as the pinnacle of human achievement. He put it at the top of his pyramid of needs (see page 35–6), saying that it could only be attempted once all the lower needs, from food to self-esteem and endorsement by others, had been met. He claimed that only 1–2 per cent of people ever attain self-actualization as most of us remain caught up in pursuing those pesky needs for food, shelter and a halfway decent car. But for Maslow, 'people' principally meant white American males of the mid-20th century, who really aren't most people (especially now). A quick look around shows many people we might feel are self-actualized without necessarily having met some of the needs further down the pyramid.

Maslow acknowledged that not all people feel the needs in the order he put them and that for some people they will be met in a different order. This is encouraging, as it means you can still aim for self-actualization if other people don't respect your views or you have a chronic health problem. Indeed, there is some contradiction between Maslow's pyramid of needs and self-actualization. What Maslow called 'belongingness' is manifested in the need for endorsement and respect from others. Yet one of the characteristics of self-actualized people that he identified was the ability to continue with unpopular views if they are securely held – so persisting in the face of no endorsement or respect lets you leap-frog a bit of the pyramid.

Are you self-actualized?

Maslow identified common features of the self-actualizers he studied. They:

- Had a realistic view of themselves and others and accepted them for what they were, tolerating flaws
- Were resourceful, independent and autonomous
- Saw reality clearly and judged situations honestly, not being easily deceived
- Were spontaneous

ROGUES' GALLERY: THE SELF-ACTUALIZED

Maslow's study of how to achieve self-actualization was based on the biographical details of eighteen people he considered self-actualized. They included:

- Abraham Lincoln – US president
- Albert Einstein – physicist; Nobel Prize winner for Physics
- Eleanor Roosevelt – political activist working for rights of women and African Americans (wife of Franklin D. Roosevelt)
- William James – philosopher and psychologist (brother of the novelist Henry James)
- Sigmund Freud – psychologist.

- Tended to be unconventional, as they didn't slavishly follow established norms and conventions
- Could tolerate uncertainty
- Needed privacy and time to themselves
- Were highly creative
- Were centred on a task or problem outside themselves
- Had an unusual sense of humour that was not at the expense of others
- Had strong ethical standards by which they lived
- Appreciated the world and viewed it with a sense of awe and wonder
- Had deep, satisfying relationships with a few key people rather than wide circles of shallow relationships
- Were concerned for the welfare of humanity
- Had 'peak experiences' (see panel).

South African leader Nelson Mandela is an example of a highly self-actualized individual whose whole life focused on the goal of freedom and equality for black South Africans.

It's likely that if you are self-actualized, you won't need to ask the question – you will already be content with who and what you are, and finding labels for it will be of no interest to you.

PEAK EXPERIENCES

Maslow identified having 'peak experiences' as a characteristic of self-actualized people. These are episodes of intense pleasure or feeling of enlightenment and insight that come about on contemplating great art, beauty in nature, or making an intellectual discovery or other personal accomplishment. They are ecstatic, transcendental and might make the person feel part of a great connectedness of nature or spirituality. The beneficial effect endures after the peak experience has finished.

Peak experiences are sometimes categorized as religious and revelatory by those who have them, and Maslow suggested that all religions have come about as the result of the peak experiences of some individual prophet or 'seer'. Pharmacological research has reproduced the peak-experience effect with the psychotropic drug psilocybin, present in 'magic mushrooms' that have been used in some religious rituals for millennia.

The path to self-actualization

Becoming self-actualized should be straightforward – after all, it only involves being yourself. Yet many of us find that very difficult to do. We are too worried about what other people think, about having to fit in, and matching the expectations of others. This feeling of belongingness is, after all, something that Maslow identified as a need.

The ecstatic frenzy of a peak experience brought on by viewing art is sometimes referred to as Stendhal syndrome, after an account left by Stendhal of his trip to Florence:

'I was in a sort of ecstasy, from the idea of being in Florence, close to the great men whose tombs I had seen. Absorbed in the contemplation of sublime beauty...

I reached the point where one encounters celestial sensations... Everything spoke so vividly to my soul. Ah, if I could only forget. I had palpitations of the heart, what in Berlin they call "nerves." Life was drained from me. I walked with the fear of falling.'

Stendhal, on viewing Giotto's frescoes in Florence, 1817

Is belongingness in conflict with the self-actualizer's need *not* to be governed by the views and expectations of others? Tension, perhaps, but not conflict. Self-actualizers can be aware of what is expected of them, but have sufficient objectivity and clarity of vision to enable them to distinguish between those expectations that are simply the result of unchallenged habit and those that are rooted in something valuable and are worth meeting.

First steps

Some steps towards self-actualization are easier to make than others. Those that don't require you to turn against the tide, but just to step outside your comfort zone, will help you to build your self-actualizing muscle. An easy first step is to work hard and with full conviction at whatever you do. Experience everything fully and be open to pleasure and wonder from small sources – a more childlike way of experiencing the world. It's easier to be cynical, to say you've seen enough sunsets, or you don't have time to stop and look at the ducks. But why reduce your enjoyment of life? It's not big or clever to disdain simple pleasures, even if most grown-ups do it.

Be open to new experiences. Consciously taking responsibility for yourself and your actions, rather than seeking somewhere else to lay the blame, might feel scary at first but will soon give you a feeling of strength. Trying new things instead of sticking to what is known and safe, even if it's just trying something different on the takeaway menu, will broaden your experiences and develop your confidence. Today, crispy garlic squid – tomorrow, extreme snowboarding and a pet scorpion.

The bigger steps

No one is going to criticize you for working hard or trying something new. The harder steps are those that will – or that you fear will – bring disapproval (or even just a raised eyebrow) from those around you.

An important step is to be honest. That's harder than it sounds, as it means giving up on playing games and acting instead in accordance with your real feelings or beliefs. Suppose everyone at your workplace is turning up earlier and

> **'There are no perfect human beings.'**
> Maslow, 1970

staying later in an effort to impress. They are not actually doing more work, they are just being seen to be there. Self-actualizers won't play this game. They will do their work efficiently and work the necessary hours to do their job well, but won't pretend to be doing more than they are doing or engage in an escalating game.

Honesty is the best policy

Self-actualization requires being honest with – and to – yourself. If there is something you always do but hate doing – whether it's visiting an unpleasant relative or cleaning the bathroom – admit that you don't like it. What would be the cost of not doing it? Perhaps the unpleasant relative dislikes the visits as much as you do. Perhaps you would rather pay a cleaner to do it than clean your own bathroom.

Even if you decide to continue – if you decided that the visits are valuable to your relative and you either can't afford a cleaner or don't approve of employing a cleaner – once you have chosen the action and taken responsibility for it, it will become easier to accept. If you are still fighting against it, you've made the wrong choice – and there is always a choice. You *could* stop seeing the relative, but you might alienate your family, lose an inheritance or feel plagued by guilt. It's still a choice. Make your choice and take responsibility for it.

Know yourself, and then be true to what you know. Perhaps you like something that others look down on, such as caravanning holidays, popular boy-bands, or cheap souvenirs. So what? Embarrassment comes with caring what other people think of your harmless choices. Work out for yourself what you think and enjoy, without deferring to the preferences of others. That's not to say you need to dismiss the opinions of others, or never listen to advice, but evaluate all that you see and hear in the light of your own experiences and tastes and make your own choices – ones that will make you happy and fulfilled.

Stand firm

The hardest step is to stand up for the things you want and believe when they are different from those that the people around you want or believe. It takes courage to stand against the tide because you think you are right, and to face hostility. You might suffer for your beliefs. If you are self-actualized, it will be worth it – because integrity will have become your greatest treasure. That's why Edward Snowden claimed he revealed the National Security Agency's secrets and had to run away to Hong Kong and then Russia. It's why Nelson Mandela and Aung San Suu Kyi spent years in jail. They believed in something greater than themselves, that was worth any risk or suffering. (Whether you or I believe they were right is not relevant.)

Self-actualizing is about *your* self

To be self-actualized, you need to know who you should be. That is, by definition, different for everyone. Someone can be lazy and rude but still self-actualized if they have been true to their own values and aims. (Diogenes might fall into that category – never doing a stroke of work.) No one can do your self-actualizing for you, or tell you who it is you should be aiming to be.

The self-actualized are also sympathetic to the needs of others to self-actualize, so they don't try to force their views on other people or mould their children to their own ambitions. Instead, they help others to find their own path and endorse brave choices even if – perhaps especially if – they are not the choices they would have made themselves.

Is it all good? Self-actualization all sounds fine and dandy, but there can be problems, as Fritz Perls pointed out. Perls,

> '*Why do we set our standard of sanity so cautiously low? Can we imagine no better model than the dutiful consumer, the well-adjusted breadwinner? Why not the saint, the sage, the artist? Why not all that is highest and finest in our species?*'
> Theodore Rozsak, Professor of History, California State University, 1977

the originator of Gestalt therapy, said there is a danger of people actualizing an ideal of the self, rather than the genuine self. We all have an idea of the type of people we want to be, and it is not always a good match for the type of person we are capable of being or suited to being. Perls felt, too, that there was a danger of self-actualization being felt as an obligation and so another pressure on the individual.

Ironically, the pressure to conform to an ideal by being self-actualized is directly counter to the requirement not to follow convention or social pressure if it doesn't coincide with your own beliefs and inclinations. It could also become a matter of morality, with us feeling that a 'better' person is self-actualized. Is that inappropriate? Is Perls just letting people off the hook if they are too lazy to improve themselves? If a person is not motivated to self-actualize, perhaps that is because either some other need has not been met or because something else is lacking. Where will

motivation come from in an unmotivated person? What if their actualized self *is* unmotivated and lazy?

Jeanne d'Arc, seen by the French as a national heroine, was certainly self-actualized. Today, she might be diagnosed as delusional and subject to hallucinations; she'd be unlikely to be given control of an army. Yet her charisma and conviction carried her through – no one says the self-actualized have to be right or sane.

Chapter 16

Carrot or stick?

Which makes human beings perform better:
the reward system or punishment?

What's the best way to get people to do something: offer them a reward or threaten a punishment? It's not just about bending others to your will – should you threaten or reward yourself?

Get motivated

Two different types of motivation might drive us to do something: internal and external.

Internal motivation is when we want to do something for our own reasons – because we enjoy the activity, find it rewarding in some way, or it builds towards goals that are valuable to us. If you like to bake, you won't need any encouragement to do it – you will be happy to do it anyway. External motivation is when we want to do something to control external circumstances – to be paid, to avoid going to jail or being hungry, and so on. If you have a job you don't much like, you will continue to turn up and do as you are told because you need the money you are paid for doing it. If you hate shopping for food, you will do it anyway because otherwise there won't be any food in the house when you are hungry.

It's the external motivation that is subject to carrot-and-stick-ness.

Too many carrots spoil the broth?

In 1973, psychologists Mark Lepper, David Greene and Richard Nisbett carried out an experiment with a group of three- to five-year-old nursery schoolchildren to test the 'overjustification' theory of reward. They selected fifty-one children who enjoyed drawing. That the children already liked the activity was key to the study. Each child was encouraged to draw for six minutes. Before starting, they were randomly put into three groups. Only one group was promised a reward (a certificate) if they did some drawing. The other two groups weren't told to expect anything. After the session, those who had been promised a certificate were given it, and one of the other groups also received a certificate. For this group the reward was a surprise. The third group received nothing.

Over the next few days, the researchers observed the children and noted how much time they spent drawing of their own volition. The results were surprising. There was no statistical difference between those given a surprise reward and those given no reward, but those given a promised reward drew *less*.

It seems that for an activity we like, internal motivation is enough. If external reward is added to that, we bump into 'overjustification'.

It appears that we generally associate external rewards with actions we don't want to do. Children might be rewarded for tidying their toys away, cleaning their room, eating their greens or doing their homework. If you plan to reward any of those, think carefully. If your children already like greens or homework, you might put them off by giving them a star chart or a pudding, because the reward suggests the task or activity was something that shouldn't be liked. After all, why would we need to be rewarded for something we are internally motivated to do?

The overjustification effect works on adults, too. People who are rewarded for giving up smoking are less successful than those who receive no reward. If their internal motivation is displaced by a less powerful external motivation, their attempt is less likely to succeed.

What lies behind this is the self-perception effect (see page 272 [*Will smiling make you happy?*]). We decide what to think about ourselves on the basis of how we behave – which sounds counterintuitive, as we would usually imagine that how we behave is manifest in how we think about ourselves.

Anyway, the children who were rewarded for drawing then had an internal explanation for their behaviour, which was that they drew because they were getting a reward, so if they were not getting a reward, they weren't going to do any drawing. Lepper's study robbed them of the joy of drawing.

Why do bankers need massive bonuses?

Most people – who are not bankers – will have wondered over the last few years why bankers are paid massive bonuses for doing a job they are already paid handsomely for. Studies of motivation and external reward show that if people are rewarded simply for completing a task, or doing it for a certain number of hours, their motivation is less than if they are rewarded for competence.

Telling someone they are being paid for doing a task well makes them work harder and longer at the task – whether or not they've actually done the task well. The reason given for paying bankers exhorbitant salaries and extravagant bonuses is that without these rewards they will leave in droves. It turns out that it's probably true. (But that doesn't answer the question of why we don't just let them leave in droves.)

That bankers persistently deny that they are the cause of the economic crash is also borne out by psychological theory.

If a person is paid more for a task, they will believe that they did it better and enjoyed it more than if they were paid badly for it. So by paying bankers large sums, we reinforce their belief that they are doing a good job and so should do more of the same. Oh dear.

HOW BORING IS THAT?

In 1959, Leon Festinger carried out an experiment at Stanford University, in California, that involved employing people to carry out a dull task. The participants were then paid either one dollar or twenty dollars to tell the waiting participants that the task was interesting. When later questioned about the task, those who were paid twenty dollars said it was boring, but those who were paid only one dollar rated it as more interesting.

Festinger's study was part of his work on cognitive dissonance (see page 263). It showed that people would persuade themselves that the task was more enjoyable than it was because they didn't want to admit they wasted their time on it and lied to the next participants. Those who were paid more had a lower view of the task. Generally, we are paid to do things we don't want to do. If we are paid a reasonable amount to do something, it's a fair bet it's something we wouldn't want to do otherwise. It's not a fun thing, so we shouldn't enjoy it. And vice versa.

Punishment works better than reward

It feels good when things stay the same. It's quite nice if they get better, but it's horrid if they get worse. (Remember the negativity bias? See page 91.) The US economist John List tried different ways of motivating teachers to coach students to pass an exam. He took similar groups of teachers and told one group they would receive a bonus if their students' test results improved. He gave $4,000 to each teacher in the other group and said they'd have to give it back if their students' grades didn't improve. On average, students of the teachers to be penalized scored 7 per cent higher than students whose teachers would be rewarded with a bonus.

CHARITY AND ANTI-CHARITY

Some people try to coerce themselves into achieving goals by pledging to give money to charity if they fail – for example, to give money to fund cancer research if they don't lose weight. This often fails. Although the incentive to keep one's money should seem a reasonable spur to action, the fact that the money is going to a good cause undermines the incentive. Giving money to worthy charities makes us feel good about ourselves and what

we have done. This means that we are setting a punishment that will make us feel good – it's not going to work. You miss your target, and think, 'Oh well, the money has gone to a good cause.'

It is much better to pledge to give to an anti-charity – a cause you don't support. It could be a political party or activist group you don't like, for instance. There is then a much more powerful incentive not to take the punishment and so to do what you set out to do.

Chapter 17

Can you spot a psychopath?

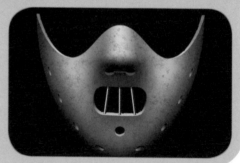

They won't necessarily be carrying an axe and gnawing on a human leg bone.

Would you know a psychopath if you saw one? Well, you probably have seen at least one. Did you notice? It's thought that around 1–2 per cent of people could be classed as psychopaths. That also means that there's a 1 per cent chance that you are a psychopath. Greetings, psychopathic readers. There's no need to worry too much – not all psychopaths turn into killers. In order for them to do so, there needs to be a particular coincidence of genes and environmental triggers.

Natural-born killers?

Jim Fallon is a psychologist who studies the brains of psychopathic killers. He has found that underactivity in the orbital cortex, a part of the brain just above the eyes, is a universal feature of the psychopathic killers he has examined. In addition, they have abnormalities in the amygdalae, two small structures located deep within the brain that are involved in regulating emotions and morality. Typically,

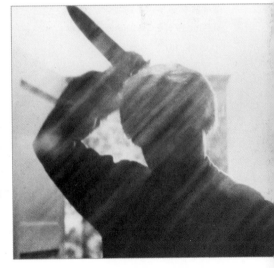

the amygdalae are underactive and around 18 per cent smaller in psychopaths. The result is that psychopaths essentially have no conscience. Although they can tell that something is wrong by comparing it with a set of moral rules, they have little or no innate sense of wrong-doing.

A bit of a shock

While working on psychopathy, Fallon was also examining PET scans of the brains of people with Alzheimer's disease. Since his mother's family had a history of Alzheimer's, he had included scans from his family members in case he might be able to spot some early signal. He was reassured to find no evidence of Alzheimer's, but the last in the pile was an obviously psychopathic brain. He assumed he had mixed up his scans. But

Lizzie Borden took an axe
And gave her mother forty whacks.
When she saw what she had done,
She gave her father forty-one.

when he checked, he discovered it was a scan of his own brain. He – the accomplished neuroscientist – had the brain of a potential psychopathic killer.

When Fallon mentioned it to his mother, she suggested he investigate his father's family. He discovered that he was directly descended from seven killers including the first man to be executed for matricide in America. Another relative was Lizzie Borden, suspected of killing her father and stepmother with an axe in 1892.

Psychopathic genes

Fallon concluded from his studies that there are several genes, called 'warrior genes', that predispose to violent psychopathic behaviour. But the carriers of these genes don't become killers unless things also go wrong in their environment. He attributed his own non-murderous life to the love of his parents. According to Fallon, those who do become serial killers have been abused or suffered other extreme trauma in childhood. Something triggers their violence beyond the genetic predisposition.

Capitalism needs psychopaths?

So what of the 1 per cent of potential psychopaths walking the streets? What are they doing? Many are successful in business. Psychopathy is over-represented amongst CEOs, with an estimated

4 per cent having psychopathic traits. Fallon is a psychopath who is a successful neuroscientist. Pro-social psychopaths, such as Fallon, have less empathy than most other people, do not form close relationships easily, and are often highly competitive, but they don't go around killing people.

When Fallon asked his friends and family what he was like, they all described him as sociopathic. He said that when he thought about it, he didn't care – and that proved they were right. A pro-social psychopath is often gregarious, hard-working, apparently sociable, but only at a fairly superficial level (so often quite charming), but not the best person to have as a close family member or close friend. Still, if they haven't suffered any childhood trauma, they probably won't take an axe to you, or their parents.

> *'Serial killers ruin families. Corporate and political and religious psychopaths ruin economies. They ruin societies.'*
> Robert Hare, University of British Columbia

On/off or a spectrum?

It's not clear whether psychopathy is a condition that people either have or don't have, or whether there is a collection of tendencies and behaviours that, in combination, result in psychopathic behaviour. If the latter, there will be a wide spectrum of psychopathy ranging from completely non-psychopathic to dangerous, criminal psychopaths.

Empathy disorders

The British psychologist Simon Baron-Cohen, an expert in empathy disorders, has noted that psychopaths are lacking in genuine empathy but are good at turning empathy on and off – they can plausibly emulate empathy while not actually feeling or acting on consideration or fellow-feeling for others. People on

Iago. Look to your wife; observe her well with Cassio.
Act III.   Scene III.

the autistic spectrum also have 'zero empathy', but they struggle with 'theory of mind' – the ability to appreciate another person's point of view or feelings. Psychopaths are very good at understanding how others think, even if they don't share their feelings. This makes them both proficient and ruthless manipulators.

Does faking madness make you mad?

The journalist Jon Ronson has studied and written about psychopathy extensively. During his research, he went

POPULAR PSYCHOPATHS

There has been some suggestion that in war zones where hostilities have continued for a long time, there may be natural selection in favour of genes that contribute to psychopathy and other tendencies towards physical aggression. The theory is that young women, when feeling physically threatened, are more likely to choose aggressive males as partners in the hope that this will keep them safe.

to meet a man called Tony who was imprisoned in the high-security mental health institution Broadmoor, in Berkshire, England. Tony told him that he had been arrested for beating someone up in a bar when he was seventeen and had been advised by another prisoner to fake madness. He would, he thought, get sent to a 'cushy' establishment instead of a real prison. Tony duly faked madness – psychopathy, in fact – borrowing ideas from films and books. He told the authorities that he got sexual pleasure from crashing cars into walls, an idea taken from the movie *Crash*. He said he wanted to watch women die as it would make him feel normal – an idea taken from the autobiography of serial killer Ted Bundy, which he found in the prison library(!). Tony was very convincing – so convincing that, instead of being sent to a cushy jail he wound up in the harshest secure institution in the land. Ooops.

Even though Tony said he had only faked madness, he spent fourteen years in Broadmoor before he was eventually released. Tony told Jon Ronson that every time he did anything normal – such as talk to a nurse about an odd news story, or wear a pin-stripe suit – it was taken as evidence of madness. The clinician told Ronson that he realized Tony had deliberately faked psychopathic symptoms – but he was so lacking in remorse and so manipulative he probably was psychopathic.

Despite his extensive studies of psychopathy, Ronson was fairly

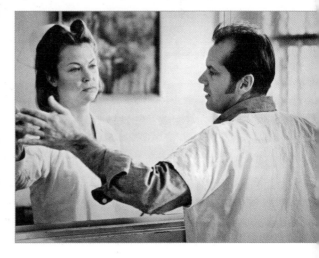

In One Flew Over the Cuckoo's Nest *(1975), McMurphy pretends to be mad to avoid hard labour.*

convinced by Tony. Did Tony manipulate Ronson into believing his story that he was not a psychopath? Or perhaps he really wasn't a psychopath. It is, as Tony found out, much easier to persuade someone that you are mad than that you are sane. A lot of the things sane people do can look mad to others.

Twenty months after his release, Tony was again jailed for attacking someone in a bar.

PSYCHOPATH-SPOTTING

There are numerous tests used to assess the degree of psychopathy displayed by any individual. One of the most widely used is the Hare Psychopathy Checklist, which lists characteristics for which the subject is rated one or two, depending on whether the feature does not apply to the subject at all, applies to some degree or is fully displayed by the subject. (You can find the test online, but for its results to be valid it must be administered by a trained psychologist. Don't act on any diagnosis or self-diagnosis you make using a web page.) Signs of psychopathy measured by the Hare checklist include:

- Glibness and superficial charm
- A grandiose sense of self-worth
- Pathological lying
- A parasitic lifestyle
- Numerous, shallow and/or short-lived sexual relationships
- Irresponsibility
- Impulsive behaviour
- Failure to take responsibility for own actions
- Lack of empathy.

Chapter 18

What do you see?

Your eyes and brain work together to see things and they don't always get it right.

You will have seen the image on page 189, or one like it, a hundred times. Why does it confuse our brains so that the image seems to jump backwards and forwards between a vase and two faces? The answer is that our minds like to work out what is the foreground and what is the background and when they can't – when both make a meaningful shape – we see something called a multistable image.

Patterning what we see

Seeing is harder than you think. Your brain has a lot to do when you look at things. All it gets is a set of data in the form of coloured light emitted or reflected by objects 'out there'. To see in

> '*Whilst part of what we perceive comes through our senses from the object before us, another part (and it may be the larger part) always comes out of our own mind.*'
> William James, philosopher and psychologist

a meaningful way, the brain needs to recognize objects, even when they are differently lit, differently oriented and different distances from the eye.

There is some debate over how much of seeing is learned and how much is innate. Experiments with very young babies (two to three months old) have shown that some features are already in place. Constancy of size (recognizing something is the same size even if it is further away), depth perception, and shape and pattern recognition are all skills that very young babies seem to have. The babies Jerome Bruner studied in 1966 (see page 287) could even make pattern-completion choices, generalizing a triangle with a bar across it to a complete triangle rather than to any other shapes that would look the same when the bar was present.

Very young babies can't actually say what they see, or even point or move towards their preferred solution. Therefore experiments with infants use constancy of gaze as a measure of interest or recognition. Babies will look for longer at something they are interested in.

Seeing and moving

Animal experiments suggest that if a young animal is not exposed to normal light and patterns, it is not able to respond normally to them later on. R. Held and A. Hein found in 1963 that if kittens could not move around in the environment, they were later unable to place their paws properly or respond to approaching objects as they could neither develop depth perception nor link coordination and perception.

Studies of people who had their sight restored after losing it as a baby, or never had sight, suggest that some aspects of vision are learned and some are innate. Cultural differences, and the environment in which people grow up, can also affect perceptual abilities. Colin Turnbull studied the Mbuti pygmies of Zaire. As they live in dense forest, he suspected they would have difficulty judging distance and size. He found that if he took Mbuti to the plains and showed them distant buffalo, they thought them 'strange insects' and were amazed that they appeared to get larger as they got nearer.

Look for the whole, not the hole

Look at this image:

Your mind organizes this design into a white triangle in front of three black circles, or a white triangle with black corners. It's unlikely you will just see three three-quarter circles. If we were to rearrange the components, however, it would be easy to see them as individual elements rather than as a single shape.

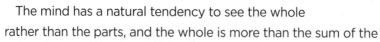

The mind has a natural tendency to see the whole rather than the parts, and the whole is more than the sum of the parts.

It's a bit like comparing a salad with its ingredients. Nothing has happened to the ingredients – it's just how they are presented. If you came to my house and I gave you an avocado, a pile of rocket, some pine nuts and a chunk of parmesan to grate over them, a bottle of virgin olive oil and some balsamic vinegar, you wouldn't be that impressed. But if I had mixed them together and made them look nice, you'd probably be quite happy with it. (If not, you aren't invited.)

Size and distance

The brain interprets the image below as a series of figures of increasing sizes from left to right, with the smallest closest to us. The lines suggesting walls and paving jog us into seeing a perspective view, with the figure on the right being the more distant. Actually,

these three figures are drawn the same size. It is your brain that does the perspective work. If one figure is in the distance, and is the same size as a figure in the foreground, we know the background figure should appear smaller. So if it appears to be the same size we interpret this as meaning the figure in the background is larger.

What's missing?

We naturally supply the missing parts to make a picture more satisfying and fit the patterns we are used to seeing. You see these shapes below as a circle and a rectangle, not lots of different lines.

But it's not just about seeing the whole. We make lots of deductions and assumptions to help us interpret what we see.

Is this next photo a zebra shape painted on a fence? Or is this the shadow of a zebra just out of shot?

Your brain uses your knowledge and past experience to interpret what it sees. A young child who had never seen a zebra-shaped animal might still guess this is a shadow of something as we are used to seeing shadows, but not used to seeing odd shapes painted on metal and wood fencing.

And what's there?

Sometimes we get it wrong. The image on page 196 of a 'face' on Mars, revealed forty years ago, had people around the world coming up with all kinds of theories about aliens having visited the planet or lived on it in the past, or gods having left imprints there. (Why would gods do that? To fool us? To encourage us in space exploration?) Yet when the same feature was imaged in 1998 from a slightly different angle and under different lighting conditions, it turned out to be just any old mountain.

The brain has to recognize general types of object so that it can identify that two are the same type of thing, even if they don't look very similar. We have no difficulty identifying human beings, even though they can be tall, short, fat, thin or whatever. Similarly we can easily recognize a tree, or a chair or a cat, even if we have never seen that particular type before.

We can also recognize the same object when seen from a different angle, distance or position.

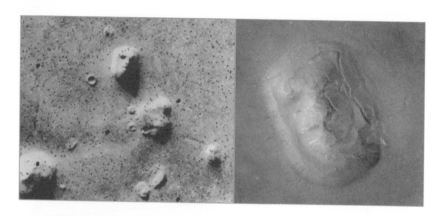

PSYCHOBABBLE: PAREIDOLIA

Pareidolia is finding significance in random or fuzzy images or sounds. The mind reinforces the familiar, struggles to find meaning, and so comes up with patterns that don't reflect reality but give us a way of interpreting what we see or hear. Pareidolia explains why people see the Virgin Mary or Allah in toasted cheese sandwiches, or a face on Mars.

And even though our depth perception is usually created using the input from both eyes, we don't see a two-dimensional image if we close one eye – our brain makes a pretty good stab at creating a three-dimensional perspective view using the input from the working eye.

No undo function

You can't undo the work your

> 'If you look at any walls spotted with various stains or with a mixture of different kinds of stones, if you are about to invent some scene you will be able to see in it a resemblance to various different landscapes adorned with mountains, rivers, rocks, trees, plains, wide valleys, and various groups of hills. You will also be able to see divers combats and figures in quick movement, and strange expressions of faces, and outlandish costumes, and an infinite number of things which you can then reduce into separate and well-conceived forms.'
> Leonardo da Vinci, *Notebooks*

brain has done in figuring out what it sees, unless a second interpretation is equally valid. Look at the image at the top of page 198.

The 'Sphinx' is a natural rock formation found in the Bucegi Mountains in Romania. The first photograph of the rocks was taken in 1900, but the Sphinx was not 'discovered' until 1936, when a picture was taken from a sideways position.

To start with, you will see a lot of black splodges. As soon as you perceive an actual image, it's very difficult to go back to seeing it as a random pattern.

Perhaps you can remember being unable to read, and seeing writing only as a bunch of squiggles. Once you can read, it's impossible to see writing as mere shapes. To recapture that feeling, you have to look at writing in a script you can't read.

Here is some text in Tamil. Unless you read Tamil, you only see it as abstract shapes:

Parts or wholes?

Gestalt theory says that we perceive things in their totality, not by putting the parts together. In the camouflaged picture of the Dalmatian above, we don't see the ears first, then the tail, then the

A and B. An object viewed from different angles. *C.* The same object distorted. *D.* The same object differently represented.

paws and deduce from this that it is a Dalmatian. We see the whole dog at once (or not at all). This is called emergence.

The white triangle in front of three black circles on page 192 is an example of reification – the way our minds create an object.

Invariance is the property that tells us that an object is the same even if viewed from a different angle or distance, or if differently represented – sometimes even if distorted.

How we pattern things

Gestalt theory suggests our minds follow certain laws that help us to impose patterns on what we see.

The law of proximity makes us see things as groups if they are close together. We see image A (next page) as three groups of twelve circles rather than just thirty-six circles.

The law of similarity states that we tend to group things if they are similar. In image B we see three rows of black circles and three rows of white circles, rather than a block of thirty-six circles.

The law of symmetry is what makes us complete a partial triangle or other unfinished shape. The law of symmetry makes us group objects by symmetry. So we see this – [ ] { } [ ] – as three sets of brackets, not six separate brackets

The law of past experience can overrule the laws in some cases. Past experience will make us see '13' as the number thirteen, unless we are looking at words in which we expect to see the letter 'B': 13BC.

The law of common fate makes us group objects if they move together or in the same direction, while the law of continuity is what makes you see the images on the next page as two lines that cross rather than four lines that meet.

The law of 'good Gestalt' says that we perceive shapes and lines

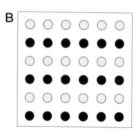

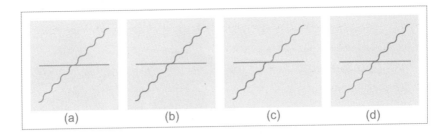

| (a) | (b) | (c) | (d) |

together if they form an object that is simple, regular and concise. Our mind tries to impose regular form on things we see. So this is seen as a square and a triangle overlapping, not an irregular shape with eight sides:

Verbatim and gist

One model of perception says we encode what we see in two ways: verbatim and gist. Verbatim refers to what the image actually shows and gist refers to the meaning we take from it. This allows us to play nasty tricks on our minds, like this... give an instant response: what colour is the text in this box (right)?

BLACK

US psychologist John Ridley Stroop took this a stage further. He discovered that if you print the names of colours in the wrong colour it took longer to read because the brain had to overcome its initial confusion. This delay in mental reaction times has since been exploited in countless psychological experiments. It is known as the 'Stroop effect'.

Bats out of hell

There is often more than one type of pattern that can be imposed on something ambiguous or incomplete that we see. Psychologists and recruitment staff often use this to gain some kind of insight into someone's preoccupations or character.
Devised by Hermann Rorschach in 1921, the Rorschach inkblot test consists of showing people symmetrical inkblots and asking them what they see. There are ten cards in the full Rorschach test.

Responses are coded and interpreted, and used to diagnose possible psychiatric conditions or indicate personality types. The test was extremely popular in the 1960s, remains so in Japan, is still widely used in the USA, but widely distrusted and barely used at all in the UK. There have been several criticisms of its validity.

Another test commonly intended to give an insight into patterns of thought, preoccupations and levels of creativity is to present someone with a shape or line and ask them to incorporate it into as many different drawings as they can. You can try it yourself. Draw as many pictures as you can using a circle in two minutes.

Chapter 19
Do violent images make you mad?

It's often said that violence on the screen leads to violent behaviour. What's the evidence?

Does viewing violence and aggression on TV, the internet and in video games really make people more violent? Or is it just that a large proportion of young men play video games, so a large proportion of young male killers will also play video games? The evidence that witnessing violence leads to violence seems compelling.

Game over

After Aaron Alexis shot twelve people dead in a naval yard in Washington DC, USA, in 2013 the popular media blamed the crime on his fondness for playing the video game Call of Duty. Anders Behring Breivik, who killed seventy-seven people in Norway in 2011, says that he practised his aim by playing Call of Duty and World of Warcraft. Adam Lanza, responsible for the shooting at Sandy Hook Elementary School, like Anders Breivik,

GTA IRL

'Life is a video game. Everybody's got to die sometime.'
Devin Moore, teenager, Alabama: arrested for a minor traffic offence, he snatched a gun from a police officer, shot three officers and stole a police car to make his getaway. He said he was influenced by playing Grand Theft Auto (GTA).

'trained' by playing Call of Duty. Seung-Hui Cho, killer of thirty-two people at Virginia Tech University in 2007, was a keen player of the violent video game Counterstrike. After nearly every mass shooting, the popular media cite corruption-by-video-game or corruption-by-movie-violence as a contributing factor.

Being mean to Bobo

In 1961, psychologist Albert Bandura set out to discover whether children copy role models who demonstrate violence. He and his colleagues at Stanford University recruited seventy-two young children, some adult researchers to act as models, and some Bobo dolls – large, durable inflatable dolls that can be knocked over but quickly spring back to an upright position.

The children were divided into equal groups of boys and girls. One group of each gender was exposed to an aggressive adult model, one to a non-aggressive adult model and there was one control group with no adult model. Individually, the children were led into a playroom with toys for them to play with in one corner, and an 'adult' corner with a mallet and peg board, and a Bobo doll reserved for use by the adults.

For the 'aggressive' groups, an adult model entered the room, played with the adult toys for one minute, then attacked the Bobo doll, hitting it with the mallet, punching it, throwing it around and

BOBO DOLL

abusing it verbally. After ten minutes the adult left. For the non-aggressive groups, the adult entered the room and played with the adult toys for ten minutes, ignoring the Bobo doll, then left. The control groups played alone for ten minutes.

Being mean to children

For all groups, the children were then individually taken to a different playroom full of interesting toys. They were allowed to play for two minutes, then the experimenter said he had decided to reserve these toys for other children and they were no longer allowed to use them. They could instead play in the experimental room. This bit of meanness was intended to generate negative feelings by making the children anxious and cross. The frustrated children were returned to the experimental room and allowed to play alone for twenty minutes, secretly observed by the experimenter.

Bandura found that the children exposed to an aggressive model were more likely to attack or verbally abuse the Bobo doll themselves. He found a significant difference between levels of aggression in boys and girls, with girls more likely to emulate a female role model and be unaffected by a male role model's aggression. Boys were three times more likely than girls to attack the Bobo doll after spending time with an aggressive role model.

Interestingly, both boys and girls exposed to a non-aggressive role model were less likely to show aggression than children in the control group. It seems that a non-aggressive role model has a positive influence.

Was it fair?

There have been criticisms of the experiment. It's not clear whether the effect of watching the adult role model would last longer than the few minutes between the stages of the experiment. Also there was no relationship or communication between the children and the adult role model, which is not typical of the children and adults interact in the real world.

There has also been a suggestion that the children were not acting out of aggression at all but out of a desire to please by emulating the adult. Finally, it has been pointed out that Bobo dolls are designed to be hit and to bounce up again, so playing with the doll like this is fun.

The behaviour of the experimenter might also have encouraged aggression: the children were deliberately frustrated and taunted,

MONSTERS UNDER THE BED?

The children in the 1961 study were too young (under eight) to be able to tell what is real from what is not. Children up to the age of twelve years might sincerely believe there are monsters under the bed. They might then be unable to distinguish between real violence and play or pretend violence. For this reason, the Committee of the Convention on the Rights of the Child (for the UN) recommends that children under the age of twelve should not be held criminally responsible for their actions, even for murder.

which might itself be considered to be modelling aggression.

Just deserts

Bandura repeated his experiment in 1963, this time with the intention of finding out how reward and punishment affect whether children emulate aggressive behaviour. Groups of children between two-and-a-half and six were shown films in which a model aggressively attacked and screamed at a Bobo doll, and then was either rewarded with sweets or punished with the warning 'Don't do it again!' For the control group, the film stopped at the end of the aggressive scene.

The children were then allowed to play in a room with a Bobo doll. Once more, there was more aggression among boys than girls, but the subsequent fate of the model also mattered. Children who had seen a film in which the aggression was rewarded were more likely to be aggressive themselves.

To test whether the children had properly observed and remembered the behaviour of the model, they were then asked to copy it. They were all able to emulate the behaviour,

> *'We went through something like 200 titles rented by the Venables family. There were some you or I wouldn't want to see, but nothing – no scene, or plot, or dialogue – where you could put your finger on the freeze button and say that influenced a boy to go out and commit murder.'*
>
> Merseyside detective investigating the murder of James Bulger, aged two, by two older children in 1993. There had been several attempts to link the murder with 'video nasties' – unclassified violent films released on video.

showing that the reward or punishment in the film had no effect on the children's learning or recall.

Real life, film and cartoons

Bandura also compared results with children who had watched a real person act aggressively, children who had watched a film of someone attacking the Bobo doll, and a cartoon cat attacking the Bobo doll. In all cases, the children who had witnessed aggression, whether actual, filmed or in a cartoon, were more likely to behave aggressively.

Tried and tested

Variations on the Bobo doll experiment have consistently come up with much the same results. When a live clown replaced the Bobo doll, the clown suffered at the hands of the children. When small children were replaced with married men, and the film of the attack on Bobo replaced with violent or non-violent TV programmes, the men who had watched violence were later reported by their wives to be more aggressive (1977). There was a similar result comparing the behaviour of people who watched a violent film or romantic movie (1992).

People set to play violent or non-violent video games also differed in their level of aggression later (2002). Those who played a violent video game were more aggressive afterwards than those who played a non-violent game.

Clearly, not all people who enjoy violent video games go on shooting rampages.

Several people who have carried out gun massacres were keen video gamers – but then, they were all young men, and many young men play video games.

The Bobo doll experiments suggest there is a link between witnessing violence and acting aggressively but this is not justification for assuming in any particular case that

> '*Exposure to violence in video games may influence the development of moral reasoning because violence is not only presented as acceptable but is also justified and rewarded.*'
> Mirjana Bajovic, Brock University, Ontario, Canada

BLAME THE BRAIN

In 2006, the Indiana University School of Medicine carried out brain scans on forty-four young people straight after they had played either a violent or a non-violent video game. Those who had played violent games showed extra activity in the amygdalae, (which, as we have already seen, are responsible for stimulating emotions) and decreased activity in the prefrontal lobe (which regulates self-control, inhibition and concentration). Those who played non-violent games showed no such changes.

Numerous studies have found that watching something violent or threatening on screen causes a rush of adrenaline – the chemical that prepares the body to fight or run away when confronted with real-life peril. The body, at least, is not able to tell the difference between real violence and fantasy violence. When neither response is needed – we rarely run away from the screen – the body is left awash with adrenaline, which might make an aggressive response to some other trigger more likely.

playing violent games leads directly to being violent.

There are also links between spending a lot of time playing video games and suffering from depression. It's not clear whether gaming causes people to become depressed or people who are prone to depression are more likely to play video games.

> *'It could similarly be argued that bread consumption predicts school shootings, because most school shooters likely consumed a bread product within 24 hours before their violent attacks.'*
> Patrick Markey, Villanova University

But he was also suffering severe mental health problems as a result of witnessing terrible scenes while involved in rescue work after the terrorist attack on the World Trade Center in New York (9/11). He had sought help with serious mental problems just one month before the shooting.

Gaming vs real life

Young teens (boys, principally) who spend many hours a day playing video games of any kind often fall behind in developing social skills because they are not interacting with people in the real world while gaming.

It's a chicken-and-egg situation: are asocial boys drawn to gaming, or do gamers fail to develop social skills, and so become asocial? A study at Brock University in Canada found that children aged thirteen and fourteen who spent three hours or more each day playing violent computer games were slower to develop empathy and a sense of moral duty towards others than children not immersed in violent games. But again – violent games might appeal more to people prone to delayed onset of empathy.

Moving on

Since Bandura's studies in the 1960s, violence in films and on TV has become even more graphic, and ever more violent video games have emerged. Violent video games are different from violent films and TV programmes in one important respect – the player is involved in perpetrating simulated violence, and not just viewing it. Are they, as some people claim, a safe outlet that allows expression of violent feelings harmlessly? Or do they lead to an increased tendency to commit violence in the real world?

There have been dozens of further studies on the impact of watching real, video or cartoon violence since Bandura's experiments more than fifty years ago. There is still no consensus.

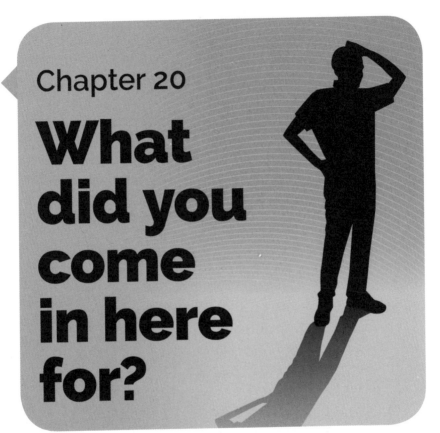

Chapter 20

What did you come in here for?

Our memories can play tricks on us – but we can
play tricks on them too.

We have all had the experience of entering a room for something and then forgetting what we went in there for. Or of being introduced to six people at a meeting or party and being unable to remember their names only a minute later. Short-term memory loss gets worse with age, but our short-term memories are not very good to start with. It's just that our memory's definition of short-term is even shorter than we think.

Do you remember when...?

We can remember some things for a split second and some for a lifetime. Many things are forgotten altogether – at least consciously. Some 'forgotten' memories can be restored with hypnosis or other help. How does memory work?

Our eyes and ears store a snapshot of incoming data for less than a second. It's possible that this is used to decide which bits need to be moved to longer-term storage and which can be ignored. After all, our brains are subjected to a constant barrage of information, most of which is not needed.

Anything that looks useful is moved into short-term memory (STM). This is the type that should let you remember you went to the kitchen to pick up a spoon, or the name of the person you just met. STM typically lasts 15–30 seconds, so if your kitchen is a long way from where you started, that's why you forgot the spoon. STM can hold around seven items. If we deliberately try to remember things for a short time, we often do it by repeating words in our heads. STM seems to be acoustic, which may be why it is harder to remember words or sounds that are similar, such as rhyming words ('bat, cat, mat, rat, hat, and fat', for example) than to remember dissimilar-sounding words ('cat, dog, ham, toad, stick and mud').

Long-term memory (LTM) can store information for a whole lifetime. 'Can' store doesn't mean it always does, as anyone who has struggled to revise for an exam will know. LTM seems to have a limitless capacity – though it doesn't always seem like it. It is semantic – it works with meaning. It's easier for LTM to store words that have

In 'Kim's game', taken from a Rudyard Kipling story, you look at a selection of items on a tray for thirty seconds and then look away and try to name them all. Most people who take part can remember between five and nine items.

similar sounds than words that have similar meanings. Often, we need to keep things in long-term memory for only a few minutes or hours. You might want to remember a shopping list until you get to the supermarket, but you won't need to recall it next year. After it's been used, you can safely forget it.

Why don't you forget how to ride a bicycle?

There are several types of memory. One, called procedural memory, is the type that's responsible for 'knowing how' to do something, such as a physical skill, and it's very resilient. Procedural memory

MEMORY TIP: CHUNKING

If you have to remember a number longer than seven digits, it's easier if you 'chunk' it. So a phone number is best remembered in pairs or triplets (or 'chunks'):

07 32 98 56 44

And is easier to remember than individual figures:

0 7 3 2 9 8 5 6 4 4

And a shopping list is easier to remember as:

Beans and bread; tomatoes and butter; coffee and milk, especially if there is some semantic meaning to the groups. (So coffee and milk is easier to remember than 'coffee and tomatoes' because people often put milk in their coffee but rarely tomatoes.)

stores all kinds of skills that, once learned, are rarely forgotten, including how to ride a bicycle. Even people who suffer anterograde amnesia, losing the ability to store long-term memories, usually remember the skills they have acquired, and can learn new skills of this type.

Other types of memory are imagery memory and declarative memory. What we see and hear forms imagery memories that we can often recall just as we first experienced them. Declarative memory is the type we most often mean when we talk about memory. It includes semantic memory, which is responsible for remembering meaning and facts, and episodic memory, which is constructed from our personal history and is linked to particular times and places.

How we remember

Although the sequence sensory memory > short-term memory > long-term memory is fairly secure, it's very clear that not all we see,

WHAT WERE YOU DOING WHEN KENNEDY WAS SHOT?

Flashbulb memories are very vivid fragments of episodic memory that burn themselves into the mind. They preserve very intense moments for us personally, or our personal circumstances – what we were doing, where we were – when some dramatic or important event occurred. That's why lots of older people can tell you exactly what they were doing when they heard President Kennedy had been shot in 1963, or Martin Luther King in 1968, and many of us can remember what we were doing when we heard about the 9/11 terrorist attacks. (Not all psychologists agree that 'flashbulb' memories are anything special. They might seem very solid just because we revisit and rehearse them frequently.)

hear or experience makes it into long-term memory. Much of our time at school is spent trying to learn and remember things; making the right choice about what to remember is vital.

A better way of looking at STM is considering it 'working memory'. If we compared it to a computer, sensory memory would supply the input from the keyboard and mouse, working memory would be RAM, and long-term memory would be the hard disk or cloud storage where we save our work.

Working memory has the task of processing incoming data and deciding whether to keep it or throw it away. Something called the 'central executive' operates as a sort of overseer or manager, juggling input and output. It can manage several tasks at once as long as they don't require the same types of skill or attention. So a person can knit and watch television, but not read and talk at the same time.

The bits and pieces that the working memory has singled out for long-term storage are best remembered if they are processed deeply. This means they must be analysed and understood, not just repeated. Repetition can work – it's how we learned the alphabet, and we don't forget it – but processes that give meaning or link new

Stephen Wiltshire is autistic. He has an astonishing ability to recall and draw an entire city skyline accurately after viewing it once from a helicopter ride.

knowledge to existing knowledge are best for forming long-term memories.

Surprise!

Things are more memorable if there is something distinctive about them. Complexity (as long as it's not so complex we don't understand) can aid recall. We are more likely to remember 'In Xanadu did Kubla Khan a stately pleasure dome decree' than 'Kubla Khan built a nice palace in Xanadu' (though the rhythm also helps). Anything distinctive is easier to remember. This book is about psychology, so you're expecting to read facts and theories about psychology. This bit is not about psychology:

In 1916, a circus owner in Tennessee executed one of his elephants, Mary, by hanging her.

He had to use a crane, and it took two attempts. She had been found guilty of the murder of a keeper – she had trampled on him after he poked her.

As you were. We'll get back to psychology now.

Things are easier to remember if they have personal relevance. So if someone told you the meaning of a new word, you might remember it. If they asked whether a word applied to you, then explained what it meant, you would be more likely to remember it. So – 'corpulent' means fat. Are you corpulent?

You might be offended by the question, but at least you will remember it. Even manufacturing a link might work. *Anagnorisis* is the moment in a play when a character discovers something that changes everything. An example of *anagnorisis* is when Oedipus discovers he has killed his father and married his mother. Have you killed your father or married your mother?

Structuring memories

If you were to throw all your belongings – books, clothes, saucepans, DIY tools, sheets, everything – into one huge box, life would be very difficult. You would have to sort through all the hammers, phone chargers and onions every time you wanted a sock. Instead, we organize our possessions.

Our memories are the same. If memory just held a vast soup of car registration numbers, family holidays, chemical formulae and statistics about World War I, it would be hard to recall anything we wanted. So instead, the brain uses schemas to structure what we know and remember. The application of schemas to the way we think was proposed by British psychologist Frederic

Bartlett in 1932 and has been widely adopted and adapted.

You could think of a cutlery tray as a schema for cutlery. New information is easier to deal with if you can fit it into an existing schema. When you get a new spoon, you know where to put it. If you want a fork, you know where to look. Information that doesn't fit into a schema might be distorted, or easily forgotten, or mis-remembered. If it's important enough, we might revise the schema, but are generally resistant to that. If someone gave you an ice cream scoop and there was no space in your cutlery tray for ice cream scoops, you might classify it as a spoon, or keep it in a different place, or decide you don't need one and get rid of it.

Not what you thought

The strong disposition of the mind to use schemas leads to our memories distorting information. It might be distorted to fit a schema when we first encounter it, and further distorted to fit better as our schemas develop and change over time. One way this manifests is through prejudice. Suppose you saw two people struggling in the street, a young man in a hoodie and an elderly woman. The elderly woman was holding a knife. You might well report later that it was the young man in the hoodie who was holding the knife because you would consider that to be the more likely scenario. Bartlett investigated the impact of schemas on reliability of memory by telling a group of students a Native American folk tale, *The War of the Ghosts* (see panel on the next page), and then having them recall and retell the tale several times over a year. They all thought they were retelling it accurately, but made changes such as

- missing out information irrelevant to them
- changing details, order and emphasis to match what seemed important to them
- rationalizing and explaining details that didn't seem to make sense
- changing the content and style to be more in keeping with the students' own cultural background.

Schemas affect our memories of situations and places, too. In 1981, Brewer and Treyens asked thirty people to wait, separately, for thirty-five seconds in a room they were told was the office of an academic. They were later asked to recall what was in the office. Most correctly recalled things they expected to find in an office, such as a desk, but forgot unexpected objects (such as pliers). Some falsely recalled objects they expected to be in an office that were not there, such as books and pens. Bizarre unexpected items – including a skull – were well-remembered.

Don't forget

We might forget things from long-term memory if there is interference from other similar information encountered earlier or

THE WAR OF THE GHOSTS

One night two young men from Egulac went down to the river to hunt seals. Then they heard war-cries, and they thought: 'Maybe this is a war-party.' They escaped to the shore, and hid behind a log. They heard the noise of paddles, and saw one canoe coming up to them. There were five men in the canoe, and they said: 'We wish to take you along. We are going up the river to make war on the people.' One of the young men said, 'I have no arrows.' 'Arrows are in the canoe,' they said. 'I will not go along. I might be killed. My relatives do not know where I have gone. But you,' he said, turning to the other, 'may go with them.' So one of the young men went, but the other returned home. And the warriors went on up the river to a town on the other side of Kalama. The people came down to the water and they began to fight, and many were killed. But presently the young man heard one of the warriors say, 'Quick, let us go home: that Indian has been hit.' Now he thought: 'Oh, they are ghosts.' He did not feel sick, but they said he had been shot. So the canoes went back and the young man went to his house. And he told everybody: 'Behold I accompanied the ghosts, and we went to fight. They said I was hit, and I did not feel sick.' He told it all, and then he became quiet. When the sun rose he fell down. Something black came out of his mouth. His face became contorted. The people jumped up and cried. He was dead.

later. This confusion increases with the volume of information rather than the passing of time, at least over relatively short periods. It's not clear whether information is actually displaced from long-term memory, or fades away, or whether we just can't access it. It's quicker to re-learn something we have forgotten than to learn something completely new, so perhaps the information is still stored but we just can't reach it without renewing some link to it.

We are more likely to remember things in roughly the same context as we first encountered or learned them. So divers who memorize a list of words underwater are more likely to recall them underwater than on land. When people train in emergency techniques, they are more likely to remember them in a real emergency if they first practised them in a simulated emergency.

Videos of re-enacted crimes often prompt the memories of witnesses who are then able to come forward with new information. The recreation of the context aids recall of the events.

Could try harder

If you really want to remember something – when revising for an exam, for instance – you will have better recall if you:

- Repeat the material, as going over it three times (at least) will help to fix it in long-term memory
- Elaborate on it, explaining it so that it makes sense to you
- Fit it into a context or schema, so that it becomes part of your knowledge base
- Memorize cues that will help you to recall it, such as making up a mnemonic or fitting words to a tune.

WHEN FORGETTING IS GOOD FOR YOU

Sigmund Freud believed a source of anxiety and distress for many people is suppressed unpleasant memories from childhood. He thought the mind deliberately forgets or represses trauma as a protective mechanism. Such forgetting comes at a cost, though. To heal the anxiety or depression it causes, patients need help from a psychotherapist to uncover and deal with the suppressed memories. There has been some disagreement about whether recalling past trauma is helpful or harmful. Also, some 'uncovered' memories might be fabrications, suggested by the process of analysis or constructed from the patient's schemas.

Chapter 21

Mind answering a few questions?

The techniques people use to get our attention are easy to spot when you know what to look for.

Lots of people are out to persuade you to do things you don't really want to do. They need to develop more and more cunning techniques as they compete for your attention and compliance. So how does persuasion work, and can it be dangerous?

Have you had an accident?

Most people are plagued by nuisance calls. The caller – working in a call centre somewhere – doesn't know you, knows little about you, but has to try to get your attention before you put the phone down. If you hang up immediately, they've lost. But if they can get you to talk at all, they're in with a chance.

They might start by being especially polite, asking if you're having a nice day. If you answer the question, you are making an investment in the call and starting to build a bond with them. It's harder to put the phone down on someone you've just responded to.

They might start with a fabricated story, 'I hear

someone in your house has had a minor accident...' Don't worry that your personal information has been leaked, or assume they have any information at all. They say that to everyone, and some of the people will have had an accident. The fact that they 'know' something about you makes you feel involved already – again, you're less likely to put the phone down. And if you haven't had an accident, the quicker you put the phone down the better as you're taking up time they could be using to sell their accident solution to someone else.

They might say they are conducting a survey and ask you to help for a few minutes. Many people like to be helpful. Many people like answering questions about themselves (that's why we fill in silly

A FOOT IN THE DOOR

An age-old technique of salespeople is 'foot in the door'. It's the same in principle as the 'will you help me with a survey?' approach. It gets its name from the door-to-door salesmen who were common in the 1950s and 60s, hawking everything from encyclopaedias to vacuum cleaners. They would, it's said, put their foot in the way of the door as the uninterested householder tried to slam it in their face. That foot gave them the chance to start their spiel and once they got going, they had a chance of a sale.

Every time you stop to talk to a researcher or charity collector in the street, stay on the phone to a cold-caller or agree to take a leaflet, you are letting someone put a foot in the door.

quizzes in magazines and on websites). As soon as you agree to answer a few questions, you're on the hook. Now you've invested in the transaction and will not want to write off the time you've put into it.

Aren't you nice?

However uninterested you are in whatever product they try to sell you further down the line, you've shown them and – more importantly – yourself that you're a helpful person. We like to think of ourselves as helpful. You feel good about yourself – you have helped this person do their job just by answering some questions. Now you feel good, and connected to the person who produced the good feeling by asking a favour of you, you won't want to spoil that good feeling by dropping out of the interaction. You will now want, even if ever so slightly, to keep it going.

Ask for a little, get a lot

A lot of persuasion plays on how we like to think of ourselves. In 1976, Robert Cialdini and David Schroeder carried out a study into charitable giving. Students working as charity collectors went door-to-door asking for donations for the American Cancer Society. Some just asked for the donation, but some added that 'even a penny helps'. They found that those who added the line about the penny collected more money. People responded by thinking, 'I can't give only a penny' and so they gave more. Being so stingy as to give only a penny didn't fit with their self-perception as kind and generous people. By prompting people to think 'I can't give only a penny', they are planting the idea that they will give something – then it just becomes a matter of how much.

Catch their interest

Another technique is to pique people's interest. In 1994, Santos, Leve, and Pratkanis set a female researcher the task of standing on a street corner asking passers-by for change. When she just asked for change, 44 per cent of people gave money. When she asked for a quarter, 64 per cent of people complied, but this rose to

75 per cent when she asked for an odd amount such as seventeen or thirty-seven cents. Because it was more unusual, the request didn't elicit an automatic response – people stopped to think, and then, having become interested, they gave.

Not that much!

The opposite of the technique of suggesting even a tiny donation is acceptable is to ask for a large favour and then, when the person refuses, ask for a smaller favour. The trick is to make the thing you *really* want the smaller favour.

Imagine you want a friend to collect your child from school one day. If you start by asking if she will take the child for the whole weekend while you go away, she's very likely to say no. But if you then ask if she will just collect him from school and bring him home, she will probably say yes. If we see someone making a concession, we are likely to make a concession in return. It's easy to manipulate this to get what you want.

If you're in a hurry, you can do both at once. It's well known that if you phrase a request in such a way that people have an easy get-out, they'll take it. So if you say, 'I don't suppose you have time to give me a lift to town?' the default answer is 'No'. If you hitch what you do want on to a request for something you don't expect, you stand a good chance of getting the lesser favour and might, if you strike lucky, get the big favour. 'I don't suppose you would like to drive me to Birmingham, but would you please give me a lift to the station so I can get the train?' might get you your lift to town.

Low-ball technique

As a sales pitch, you'd think the opposite of reducing the request – increasing the request – would be a disaster. But, surprisingly, it works. It's typically associated with car sales. You show interest in a car, you're told the price, you decide to buy it. Then all the extras creep in, the price rising and rising. You still buy the car. Budget airlines do it, too. You've clicked on the tickets you want, and suddenly all kinds of supplements and optional extras start to appear, pushing the price up. In both cases, if we feel we've made a commitment, we follow through.

Forbidden fruit and reactance

Sometimes we don't want to persuade people to do or want something, we want to persuade them *not* to do or want something. It can be very hard to do, since as soon as something looks forbidden or dangerous, we want it. We don't like restrictions on our actions, and anything that looks like a restriction can produce a 'reactance' response – a reaction against the request or advice.

Brad Bushman and Angela Stack researched the impact of warning

and information labels on how people responded to violent TV programmes and high-fat foods.

There are two possible, conflicting responses to warning labels. 'Tainted fruit' theory suggests we will avoid high-fat food that is explicitly labelled as bad for us, while 'forbidden fruit' theory suggests we want what we think we shouldn't or can't have. The researchers investigated the different effects of no labelling, information labels (which just gave facts) and warning labels (which gave facts and pointed out risks). They found that for high-reactance individuals, the warning labels were attractive. They were more likely to want to watch a violent programme or eat a high-fat food labelled with warnings than one just giving information. An information label trusts you to use your judgment, but a warning label tells you what to do, and we don't like that.

Chapter 22

Does power corrupt?

It's easy to assume you would be a benign leader if you're never given the chance to prove otherwise.

We see it again and again. Someone seems honourable when they enter public office but within a short space of time they are acting like a corrupt tyrant. (Yes, we're looking at you, Robert Mugabe.) Apparently decent soldiers head off to war and within weeks they're napalming innocent villagers, raping young girls, manning the gas chambers or torturing Iraqi prisoners. Are they the few bad apples that spoil the barrel, as US Secretary for Defense Donald Rumsfeld said (of Abu Ghraib)? Or is the barrel spoiling the apples?

Recruiting prisoners

When Phil Zimbardo set up an experiment at Stanford University into the behaviour of people put into the roles of prison guard or prisoner, he intended it to last two weeks. He wanted to find out how positions of authority or subservience affect behaviour. As he termed it, if you put good people into a bad situation, what do they do? In the end, he curtailed the experiment after only six days as the effects on his subjects were intolerable.

Zimbardo's experiment was conducted in 1971, ten years after Stanley Milgram's chilling findings on obedience (see page 136). Zimbardo advertised in the press for volunteers to take part in a psychology experiment into the effects of prison life. Of the seventy volunteers, he chose twenty-four who were deemed fairly sane and normal and not at risk of psychological damage, and randomly assigned them to the role of guard or prisoner. All were male students from the USA or Canada.

Playing the game – prisoners

The experiment started with realistic scenarios of arrest. The police (who were cooperating with the experimenters) arrived at the homes of 'prisoners' early one Sunday morning, searched and handcuffed them, bundled them into police cars and drove them away, often under the gaze of neighbours who assumed the whole thing was

Police and guards wear sunglasses so that suspects can't see them properly or make eye contact. It increases a sense of isolation and prevents suspects forming any kind of bond with them.

real. It was a high-stress start, emulating the experience of many real suspects as closely as possible.

The 'prisoners' were taken to a real police station, booked by real police officers wearing sunglasses, and then fingerprinted, photographed, blindfolded and left in a cell.

The 'prison' was an adapted corridor in the psychology department on the Stanford University campus. Ordinary lab doors were replaced with doors with steel bars, and the 'exercise yard' was the closed corridor. There were no windows or natural light, and no clocks. Prisoners were escorted to and from the toilet as necessary. A cupboard, dubbed 'the hole' and just large enough for a prisoner to stand upright in, was available for solitary confinement. It was 60cm square. As each prisoner arrived, he was told of the severity of his crime, stripped, searched and sprayed with de-lousing spray. It sounds barbaric, but it was copied from procedures in a jail in Texas.

Each prisoner was dressed in a smock, with his prison number on the front and back. He was allowed no underclothes. That part was not copied from common prison practice, but was calculated to produce a similar level of humiliation and dehumanization as routine prisons. He wore a chain around one ankle at all times. Again, most American prisoners were not chained at that time. Instead of having his head shaved (as prisoners did), each man had to wear a cap made of a cut-down stocking. Prisoners were referred to, and had to refer to each other, by number and not by name. Prisoners slept three to a cell in barren rooms with only space for their three beds.

Playing the game – guards

Guards were given no special training, but were told to use whatever methods seemed reasonable and necessary to maintain order in the prison. They were warned of the seriousness of their position and the dangers involved. Guards wore identical khaki uniforms and mirrored sunglasses. They had a whistle around their necks, and 'billy clubs' (batons) borrowed from the police. Nine guards worked in shifts, three on shift at a time, looking after nine prisoners split between three cells. The extra guards and prisoners were on standby in case of need.

Playing the game – prison life

At 2.30am on the first night, the prisoners were awakened by a whistle and had to leave their cells for a 'count'. Counts happened

regularly thereafter, day and night, as a way of getting guards to assert authority over prisoners. Guards were allowed to punish prisoners if they disobeyed orders or rules. One common punishment was forcing prisoners to do push-ups. Zimbardo noted that Nazi concentration camp guards had also ordered prisoners to do this. One of Zimbardo's guards stepped on the prisoners' backs while they did push-ups, or made other prisoners sit or step on the backs of their fellows.

Rebellion

The first day, prisoners were compliant. The second day, they rebelled. They tore off their caps and the numbers from their gowns, barricaded themselves in their rooms and taunted the guards. The guards called on reinforcements and let off fire extinguishers at the prisoners to drive them away from the doors. (The fire extinguishers were intended for fire-fighting and not supplied for use as weapons.)

The guards opened the cell door, stripped the prisoners naked and forced the ringleader into solitary confinement. They harassed the other prisoners.

Privilege vs punishment

The team realized that they couldn't keep on using nine guards to control nine prisoners as they had needed to do in order to put down the rebellion. So the guards met and decided on methods of psychological, rather than physical control. The three prisoners least involved in the rebellion were moved into a 'privilege cell', given back their clothes, and given special food in front of other prisoners who were not allowed to eat at all. A little later, some of the 'good'

and 'bad' prisoners were swapped around, without explanation. The aim was to break solidarity between the prisoners – divide and rule, in other words. It worked. The prisoners became distrustful of each other, suspecting that some of the swapped 'bad' prisoners had acted as informants. Similar techniques,

often making use of racial tension, were employed in real American jails at the time, according to the ex-convict consultants employed to advise the experimenters.

As well as breaking solidarity between the prisoners, the response to the rebellion built solidarity between the guards, who now saw the prisoners as a threat to themselves as a group. They started to control the prisoners more rigorously, withholding toilet visits, then not allowing prisoners to empty the slop buckets they were forced to use, and controlling access to cigarettes, which distressed heavy smokers.

Breaking down

Only thirty-six hours after the start of the experiment, one prisoner started to break down. He acted irrationally, cried uncontrollably, and went into a rage. The prison consultant criticized the prisoner

ALL TOGETHER NOW...

When parents were allowed to visit their sons, they immediately fell into the role of compliant middle-class adults, making formal complaints about the treatment of their children but acting with deference towards figures of authority. They knew it was an experiment, and although they had not personally agreed to be part of it, they played the role the situation assigned them.

for being weak and explained the sort of abuse he could expect if he were a genuine prisoner. He was offered the chance of leniency in exchange for becoming an informant. It took a little while, and a lot more irrational behaviour, before the experimenters realized the man was in genuine distress and was removed from the experiment. The experimenters were later startled to see that their own thinking had become attuned to the prison situation – they had assumed he was trying to con them and had not recognized genuine distress.

It wasn't just the prisoners who started to break down, or even just the experimental subjects. The experimenters, too, were losing sight of who they actually were and slipping into the role of prison superintendents too thoroughly. When rumours of a planned mass break-out began, the experimenters should have watched it with interest, noting the pattern of behaviour. Instead, they consulted with experts on prison security and worked out a plan to foil it. When Zimbardo asked the local police if he could move his prisoners into real holding cells for the night of the planned escape, they refused. He reacted angrily at their lack of cooperation.

He chained the prisoners together, put bags over their heads and moved them to another area, then sat in the empty jail himself, waiting to confront the people who were going to spring his 'prisoners'. A fellow psychologist passed by and saw him. He asked about the experiment, and then asked what the independent variable

> *'I got really angry at him. Here I had a prison break on my hands. The security of my men and the stability of my prison was at stake, and now, I had to deal with this bleeding-heart, liberal, academic, effete dingdong who was concerned about the independent variable! It wasn't until much later that I realized how far into my prison role I was at that point — that I was thinking like a prison superintendent rather than a research psychologist.'*
>
> Phil Zimbardo, experimental psychologist

was. Zimbardo became angry – he had more important things to deal with. It was much later that he realized the experiment had got to him, too.

As it turned out, the break-out had been merely a rumour. Frustrated at their waste of time and their humiliation, the guards harassed and punished the prisoners in retaliation (retaliation for not trying to escape!). They made them clean toilet bowls with their bare hands, perform humiliating acts, including simulated sodomy, and do strenuous exercise.

The game's up

Zimbardo held parole hearings for prisoners who thought they should be eligible for parole. Two remarkable things happened. The ex-convict consultant who acted as head of the parole board acted

– to his own horror – just like the man who had refused his own requests for parole for sixteen years. And the prisoners, when asked if they would surrender the money they had earned so far in the experiment in exchange for parole, mostly said they would – but then obediently returned to their cells while their appeals for parole were considered. Any of them could have opted out of the experiment immediately (forfeiting their fee), but they acted like real prisoners. It simply didn't occur to them to quit the experiment.

The experiment came to an end when a female psychologist visited the experiment and – alone of fifty external visitors – expressed horror at the way the young men were being treated. Zimbardo realized she was right, and halted the experiment. It had done only six of its scheduled fourteen days. Later, Zimbardo said they should have stopped earlier, after the second breakdown, but even the experimenters had been drawn in and taken over by their roles as prison officials. Scary stuff.

Bad apples or bad barrels?

Zimbardo noted that there were three types of guard by the end of the period:

- Tough but fair guards treated the prisoners according to the rules
- 'Good guy' guards did little favours for

prisoners and never punished them

- 'Bad guy' guards were vindictive, sadistic, and inventive in the forms of humiliation and punishment they came up with. They seemed to relish the power they held over the prisoners and wielded it at every opportunity. Hidden cameras revealed them abusing prisoners at night, for no particular reason, when they thought they were unobserved.

Zimbardo found nothing in the profiles of the 'good guys' or 'bad guys' that could have led him to predict which they would be. The prisoners, too, fell into groups. Some were very compliant, keeping out of trouble by obeying instantly. Some put up a fight. There were more hints from the profiles this time of how people would behave. Those used to a more disciplined life were better able to withstand the pressures of being a prisoner and held out for longer than the others. One developed a psychosomatic rash over his body when his appeal for parole was turned down. Four broke down. The group dynamic between prisoners broke down completely.

A foreshadowing of Abu Ghraib

Zimbardo has noted the similarities between his experiment and the prisoner abuse in the US military prison Abu Ghraib in Iraq. In fact, some of the similarities are quite startling – stripping prisoners, making them stand with bags on their heads, and making them fake humiliating sexual acts were tactics used in both Stanford and Abu Ghraib. The abuse in Abu Ghraib was blamed on 'a few bad apples', but Zimbardo has argued that it is not the case that bad apples spoil the barrel, but that perhaps that bad barrels spoil the apples. The situations we put people in can either make them – or allow them to – do bad things.

Years after the experiment, Zimbardo spoke as an expert witness at the trial of the Abu Ghraib guards. Of course, the guards in Abu Ghraib really were under stress – they were in a conflict situation, dealing with people they believed wanted to kill them. But the 'guards' in Stanford had no such excuse. When the experiment was suspended, the prisoners were – unsurprisingly – pleased. Many of the guards, though, were disappointed. Even among the 'good' guards, none had objected to the way prisoners were being treated. No one except the lone visiting female psychologist had sounded a note of dissent on behalf of the prisoners (Zimbardo married her).

> *'I don't regard it as an experiment or a simulation because it was a prison run by psychologists instead of run by the state. I began to feel that that identity, the person that I was that had decided to go to prison was distant from me — was remote until finally I wasn't that, I was 416. I was really my number.'*
> 'Prisoner Number 416', a volunteer in the Stanford Prison Experiment

The power of evil?

The experiment would not be allowed now. It would not pass an ethics committee. There was danger of serious psychological damage to both prisoners and guards – and, as it turned out, to the experimenters, who became so caught up in their own experiment that even they lost sight of its fiction.

It might seem that this is similar to Milgram's experiment (see page 136), but there are significant and chilling differences. Milgram's experiment tested whether people would obey others and inflict harm – whether we can be enlisted into cruelty when there is a figure of authority taking responsibility for the outcomes. It's bad enough that people are willing to deliver near-fatal electric shocks to innocent others just because they are told to.

The Stanford Prison Experiment

August 15-21, 1971

But the Stanford Prison Experiment was even more disturbing. Zimbardo has used the word 'evil' to describe what people would do to one another. The title of his book about the experiment is uncompromising:

> *'If only there were evil people somewhere insidiously committing evil deeds, and it were necessary only to separate them from the rest of us and destroy them. But the line dividing good and evil cuts through the heart of every human being.'*
>
> Alexander Solzhenitsyn, *The Gulag Archipelago*, 1973

The Lucifer Effect: Understanding How Good People Turn Evil. The experiment uncovered a dark aspect of human nature – the willingness to harm others for no good reason at all, even to think up extra ways to dominate and hurt them, simply because a position of power enables it.

No one knows it's you

One of Zimbardo's conclusions was that depersonalizing individuals and hiding their identity makes the descent into pathological compliance or despicable cruelty easier and more likely:

'When people feel anonymous in a situation, as if no one is aware of their true identity (and thus that no one probably cares), they can more easily be induced to behave in antisocial ways.'

The kind of abusive trolling we see in social media, where people can hide behind an anonymous user name and don't have to confront the victims they are abusing, is a result of the same effect.

Deindividuation works both ways. The prisoners, stripped or uniformed, with heads shaved or hidden, are no longer human individuals with whom we can empathize. People are easily persuaded they are different, worthless, not deserving of decent treatment. If that can happen even among American college students over a period of thirty-six hours, how much more likely is it to happen in a war or other stressful situation?

Just as the guards are protected by their deindividuation, their mirrored glasses and uniforms masking their personal identities, the prisoners are made vulnerable by theirs. Zimbardo has said that in these situations, past and present disappear

'Any deed that any human being has ever committed, however horrible, is possible for any of us – under the right circumstances. That knowledge does not excuse evil; it democratizes it, sharing its blame among ordinary actors rather than declaring it the province of deviants and despots – of Them but not Us. The primary lesson of the Stanford Prison Experiment is that situations can lead us to behave in ways we would not, could not, predict possible in advance.'
Phil Zimbardo

and only the gratification of the moment counts. People do things without considering the consequences or the reasons. And no one can say that he or she would not do it. That is why it's so frightening.

Chapter 23

Why don't you just get on with it?

Is there something else you should be doing
instead of reading this book right now?

Procrastination. We all do it. There is a task to do, but we just can't or won't settle to it. It doesn't even need to be a boring or unpleasant task – it can still seem nearly impossible to stop wasting time and simply get on with the work or chore that is so important or urgent. Why do we persistently make life difficult for ourselves by putting things off?

DISPLACEMENT ACTIVITY

Doing something else instead of the thing you intended to do or ought to do is called 'displacement activity'. It's not just humans that do it. Animals engage in displacement activity when they can't choose between two actions, or when an action they are strongly motivated to perform is blocked.  Some birds will uselessly peck at the grass when confronted with an opponent: they can't decide whether to fight or flee, and instead do something entirely useless in the situation. We sometimes scratch our heads when trying to make a choice – that's a displacement activity. Some people chew or twirl a lock of hair or fiddle with their pen when under pressure or when wrestling with a decision or problem. These are displacement activities.

Sometimes we procrastinate until there is barely enough time left to complete the task and then work better under the pressure we have created. Sometimes we genuinely need to rest, or need down-time for our brains to work subconsciously on a problem.

> *'[Procrastination is] to voluntarily delay an intended course of action despite expecting to be worse off for the delay.'*
> Piers Steel, University of Calgary

Is it about doing it right?

It's a common misconception that procrastination is a product of perfectionism – that we put off starting something because we fear we won't do it well enough. In effect, this means we are delaying or avoiding disappointment or frustration by sabotaging the task. It's easier, in terms of one's self-image, to feel that you *could* have done well if you'd tried, than to accept that you tried your best and just weren't up to scratch. Of course, sabotaging the task also means sabotaging any possibility of succeeding at it. But studies suggest that there is in fact *no* link with perfectionism and, if anything, perfectionists procrastinate less than non-perfectionists.

Instead, procrastination correlates strongly with conscientiousness – and, curiously, with being a night owl rather than a lark. Procrastinators have less focus on the future, and have a more fatalistic and hopeless view even of the present. It seems as though there is just no point in getting on and doing things because it's not going to work out well anyway.

Feel-good factor

That all sounds rather pessimistic. But procrastination gives us some benefit to offset the longer-term loss. It gives us an immediate boost – we feel good because we are not doing a task we weren't looking forward to. It's a bit more complicated than it sounds.

Most of us, with a less-than-optimal dose of willpower, prefer instant gratification over delayed gratification, even if the instant gratification is of a lesser order. It's the 'bird-in-the-hand-worth-two-in-the-bush principle'. If you ought to wash the car, write a report or put the shopping away, it's easy to defer the task in favour of watching TV or surfing online. You will probably promise yourself that you'll do the dreary task in an hour, or tomorrow. So you feel better immediately because you are doing something you'd rather do, and you also feel better because you have planned to get the task done. You can imagine a future in which the task is done, because it will be done after the time you have set for it. Further, we are very bad at what psychologists call 'affective forecasting' – imagining how we will feel at some point in the future. So if you plan to write your report tomorrow, you feel happier because you don't have to do it now, and you anticipate that you will feel similarly happy about the plan tomorrow, when you actually have to do the task. Sadly, you won't.

Just for kicks

Some people routinely leave tasks until they can only just

EARLY TO BED...

'Early to bed and early to rise, Makes a man healthy, wealthy and wise.'
This old adage is borne out by research that shows that people who go to bed early and get up early (larks) are less prone to procrastination. As a result, they get more done and so they might well be wealthier, but are certainly wiser in terms of how they use their time. They will probably have better mental health, too, as procrastinators experience a higher level of stress and anxiety overall than non-procrastinators.

DON'T EVEN START

Procrastination through the ages: A definitive history, supposedly written by Paul Ringenbach in 1971, was never actually published. In fact, it was never even started – the whole project was a joke: a book about procrastination that he couldn't be bothered to write – but it has still ended up in a few references and bibliographies!

complete them in time. Do they get a kick out of the adrenaline rush that comes with the stress of struggling to meet an imminent deadline? Dr Joseph Ferrari of DePaul University, Chicago, Illinois, found that procrastinators had two tendencies: either they were delaying a task because they just didn't want to do it, so it was ordinary avoidance behaviour, or they delayed the task because they genuinely believed they worked better under pressure and were waiting until the point when the task really had to be started if it was to be completed at all. He concluded this second group were seeking the thrill of the stress they put themselves under. But later studies have suggested this is not the real *reason* for procrastination – it's just the rationalization for it.

Studies by Kyle Simpson at Carleton University, Ottawa, Canada,

THE OPPOSITE OF PROCRASTINATION

Procrastinators can't get going on a task, and when they do tackle it they are often disengaged and do it half-heartedly. The opposite is to experience 'flow' or to be 'in the zone'. 'Flow', as defined by Hungarian-born psychologist Mihaly Csikszentmihalyi, 'is being completely involved in an activity for its own sake. The ego falls away. Time flies. Every action, movement and thought follows inevitably from the previous one, like playing jazz. Your whole being is involved, and you're using your skills to the utmost.'

found no correlation between people who are thrill-seekers and procrastination measures. Instead, it seems that people believe, or tell themselves, that they procrastinate because they work better under pressure or enjoy the rush, but in fact that is just a way of excusing their lack of action to themselves. Few people, when doing a task at the last minute, are still glad they left it so late to start. Many regret the delay, saying they could have done a better job if they had had more time, or that they are interested in the task and it's a shame they don't have time to enjoy it properly.

Blame your brain

A tendency to procrastinate has been linked with damage to or low activation of the prefrontal cortex. This area of the brain plays an important part in planning, impulse control and filtering out distracting stimuli from other parts of the brain.

Most of us, though, don't have a damaged or underactive prefrontal cortex and so we can't use that excuse. Most of us are 'short-termists' and will delay a challenging, dull or long task to do something immediately rewarding – even if it is of little or no long-term value. Most of us procrastinate because we are lazy, lack willpower and are unmotivated. It's just hard to admit that – and if we admitted it, we might feel that we actually had to tackle it. And we really can't be bothered.

Chapter 24

Who cares if you're outbid on eBay?

Our brains have tricks to make us want what we get even if we don't get what we want.

Imagine: You are watching a major international sporting event, rooting for your national team. Then a player on the opposing team performs a truly brilliant move. You applaud. But, wait... you want him to lose. No – how can you want him to lose when he's so good? You have always mocked food-snobs

> '*If a person is induced to do or say something which is contrary to his private opinion, there will be a tendency for him to change his opinion so as to bring it into correspondence with what he has done or said.*'
> Leon Festinger and James M. Carlsmith, Stanford University, California

A person's belief that they should look after the environment might be in conflict with their desire for a fuel-hungry car. They might either not buy the car, or salve their conscience by sometimes using public transport, or rationalize to convince themselves the car is not as big an environmental threat as they once thought.

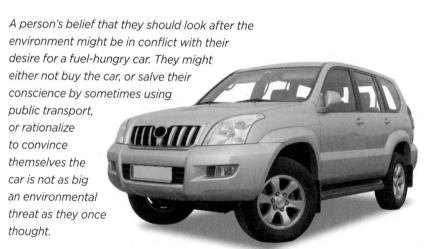

who frequent ridiculously overpriced restaurants. But then someone offers to take you out for a meal at the nearest Michelin-starred establishment. It's against your principles, but you'd love to go, just to try it, just the once... If you've have had an experience like this, you've known cognitive dissonance, described by Leon Festinger in the 1950s.

The 'boring task' experiment

In 1959, Leon Festinger and James Carlsmith carried out an experiment into how people struggle to reconcile a conflict between their actions and their beliefs. They recruited some students to carry out a task, telling them it was part of a psychology experiment into 'measures of performance'. The students were told that two groups of people were doing the experiment and one group had been briefed in advance to give them specific expectations of the task. But in fact that was a bit of a lie, and the real experiment came after the task.

The tasks were dull. For half an hour, the students had to move some spools around in a box. Then they had to spend half an hour moving wooden pegs around a board. At the end, the experimenter thanked each student, and said that many people had found the tasks interesting.

Just after, the experimenter returned. Affecting embarrassment and confusion, he told the student the person briefing the next batch of students hadn't turned up, and asked them to stand in. All they had to do was tell the next person that the task was really quite interesting. Some people were paid one dollar to do this; others were paid twenty. Afterwards, the experimenter again said that many people found the task interesting and they hoped the student had enjoyed it.

Was it really that boring?

There followed an interview about the experiment. One of the questions the interviewer asked was how enjoyable the task was. Remember, the task was really, really boring – but both the experimenter and the students themselves had said it was fun. What was really interesting,

> *'Humans are not a rational animal, but a rationalizing one.'*
> Leon Festinger

though, was that the students who were paid only one dollar to lie about the task rated it as more interesting than those who were paid twenty dollars to enthuse about it.

Festinger and Carlsmith explained this result in terms of cognitive dissonance. The students who had been paid twenty dollars felt they had been paid well enough for lying. They had been adequately rewarded for compromising themselves, and saw it as a fair trade. But the students who had only been paid one dollar didn't have this consolation. They either had to admit to themselves that they had lied for a small reward, or they had to change their evaluation of the task. It was preferable to admit they had been wrong in their opinion of the task – it wasn't *that* boring, after all. Essentially, they needed a way to salvage their dignity and the way they picked was to revise their original experience.

Join the club

It's well known that the harder it is to get into a club, the more membership is prized. Even though the club might actually be pretty mediocre, and certainly offer no better facilities than many other clubs, we justify to ourselves the effort we had to make by convincing ourselves that the club is fantastic. In 1956, Elliot Aronson and Judson Mills required people to perform either a humiliating task or a mildly embarrassing task to join

EXCLUSIVE CLUBS FOR PIGEONS?

There have been other explanations of this result, including that the level of contrast between the effort and the reward influences the participants' level of satisfaction. This interpretation is upheld by a study reported in 2007 that showed pigeons behave in the same way. If they have to work harder to get food by one means than another, they prefer the harder method. Either pigeons experience cognitive dissonance, or the reward/effort contrast is a motivating factor.

Groucho Marx reportedly sent a telegram to the Friar's Club, Beverly Hills, that read: 'PLEASE ACCEPT MY RESIGNATION. I DON'T WANT TO BELONG TO ANY CLUB THAT WILL ACCEPT PEOPLE LIKE ME AS A MEMBER.' The joke is about cognitive dissonance. He wants to join an exclusive club, but has low self-esteem. If the club will accept his membership, it can't be as exclusive as he thought, so he doesn't want to join.

a discussion group about sex. The group turned out to be very dull (a discussion about sexual behaviour in animals), but those members who had undergone the more strenuous initiation enjoyed it anyway. They needed to persuade themselves their effort had been worthwhile.

Just drink the beer and eat the doughnuts

Few of us have to lie about the boringness of a task (unless perhaps we spend our lives conducting recruitment interviews), but there are plenty of opportunities for cognitive dissonance in everyday life. We might decide to lose weight or eat healthily, but still buy doughnuts in the supermarket. We might resolve not to drink so much, and then buy another bottle of wine. This is dissonance between beliefs and behaviours. We might also have dissonant behaviours – buying a rowing machine on the same shopping trip as buying the doughnuts, for example.

Fun toys and rubbish toys

Apparently, it's not only adults who need to rationalize to explain their behaviour to themselves. Carlsmith was involved in another study, this time in 1963 with Elliot Aronson, investigating cognitive dissonance in young children. In each experiment, a child was left in a room with lots of toys, one of which was extra special. The child was told to play with any of the other toys, but that they would be punished if they played with the special one. Half of the children were threatened with a serious punishment, and half with a mild punishment. None of the children played with the special toy.

Next, all the children were allowed to play with any toy, all prohibitions lifted. The children who had been threatened with a mild punishment were much less likely to play with the very special toy than the other children. Carlsmith and Aronson explained it by saying that the children had to rationalize their self-policing response to the mild threat, and did so by persuading themselves that the toy was not really especially interesting anyway. As a result, they didn't want to play with it when they were allowed to.

In a variant of the study in 2012, four-year-old children were put in the same situation, but some of them were played classical music during the play sessions. Those that heard the music did not devalue the special toy. It seems that music, and some other external stimuli, prevents strategies that reduce dissonance.

'Well, I didn't want it anyway...'

Cognitive dissonance is behind quite a lot of our seemingly petty behaviour. For example, you are outbid for an item in an online auction. You then rationalize the situation, feeling relieved that you didn't have to spend the money, or convince yourself that you didn't really want it that much anyway. That's the same process at work: to remove the dissonant thoughts of disappointment, we immediately devalue the thing that has been lost.

When we have to choose between two items or actions, even if

the choice seems difficult at the time, we often feel much more confident with the choice as soon as it's made. The mind reinforces the choice to avoid dissonance.

It's not only people that do this kind of rationalization. In a study in 2007 that used both pre-school children and capuchin monkeys, both groups of subjects behaved in the same way. Offered two choices, then a new choice that involved the rejected item and a new item of identical

In Aesop's fable, the fox that can't reach the grapes eventually decides that they are probably sour – not worth having.

appeal, both children and monkeys chose the new item. There was clearly something wrong with the rejected item, because they'd rejected it. Why would they want it the second time round?

Catastrophe – the world didn't end!

Those of us who don't belong to fanatic religious sects built around the belief that the end is nigh quite enjoy laughing at the prophesies of doom that pop up every now and then. Festinger (again) and some colleagues decided to study the effects on cult members when these predicted doomsdays came and went without Armageddon occurring.

They studied a group called the Seekers who had believed the world would be destroyed by a great flood on the morning of 21

December 1954. Needless to say, it wasn't. The group, led by one Marian Keech (actually Dorothy Martin) who claimed to receive messages from a planet called Clarion, prepared to be whisked away in an alien spaceship before the flood.

Members had shown considerable commitment, moving

from their homes, selling their possessions and leaving their jobs and partners. The day before, they divested themselves of metal objects, and waited for an alien visitor who was supposed to arrive at midnight and lead them to the spaceship. Midnight came and went with no alien visitor. How could they respond?

It's all good...

At 4am, as they all sat in stunned silence, Keech received a message from the aliens saying that God had decided to spare the Earth – that their little group had averted the disaster. The next day, the previously publicity-shy group called all the papers to tell how they had prevented the catastrophic flood. Unimpressed, the authorities in Chicago threatened Keech with arrest and committal to a mental institution.

As Festinger predicted, the failure of the world to end did not destroy the cult but made it stronger in its proselytizing activity. Instead of realizing that their prophesy was wrong, the members adjusted what had happened to fit their beliefs – the world *had been* going to end, but their own personal goodness had averted the disaster. The cult was, then, super-good as it had done such a powerful thing, and so they could be even more confident in their commitment to it and continued to recruit new members. Cognitive dissonance wins the day!

Chapter 25

Will smiling make you happy?

Smiling is supposed to make us all feel better.
Can it be true?

If you smile, you'll feel better, people say. It sounds stupid. We smile when we are happy – we aren't happy because we smile. The things that are wrong in your life won't be fixed by you smiling. But is it really stupid, or is there some kernel of truth there? Psychologists think there might be something in it after all.

How do you know what you're like?

We decide what other people are like by watching what they do and listening to what they say. If we see someone pause to give money to a beggar in the street, stop to speak to an elderly neighbour or pick up something a stranger has dropped, we assume they are kind, thoughtful, or generous. These are the actions of a kind person, an empathic person, a generous person. On the other hand, if we see someone barge through a crowd, swear at a noisy child or get impatient when an elderly

> '*Sometimes your joy is the source of your smile, but sometimes your smile can be the source of your joy.*'
> Thich Nhat Hanh, Zen master

person holds them up by moving slowly, we form a negative opinion of them.

If we form a view of other people by their behaviour, perhaps we might form a view of ourselves in the same way. This is called self-perception – the idea that our view of who we are is informed by what we do. We observe ourselves and come to conclusions about our own character, mood and attitudes on the basis of what we see. It sounds ridiculous. Surely the way we act manifests how we are, not the other way round?

In 1972 social psychologist Daryl J. Bem, of Cornell University, New York, proposed this theory of self-perception as an alternative to the theory of cognitive dissonance. It has its critics, but at the moment it looks as though both theories have a lot to commend them, affecting people at different times. Self-perception might help people form their view of themselves, and then cognitive dissonance arises if they have to act in a way that contradicts the view they have formed. Self-perception seems to be able to sway our view of ourselves when we haven't invested a lot already in a particular attitude.

'I'm a person who does this'

If we watch what we do and then assume we are the kind of person who does that sort of thing, it should in theory be easy to change attributes we don't like about ourselves. In practice, it can

ACT DIFFERENTLY TO BE DIFFERENT

French existential philosopher Jean-Paul Sartre believed that we make choices about how we are and what we are all the time. A person is defined by what they do, and by that alone. If someone acts in a cowardly way, that makes them a coward. If they stop acting in that way and act bravely, they are no longer a coward but now a brave person. We might have an inclination to act one way or another, built up either through past experiences or genetics, but nothing compels us to act or carry on acting like that. It's both a liberating philosophy and a burdensome one – there is no one else to blame for how you are.

make it more difficult, as we tend to believe that behaviours are more ingrained than they are – they are not just behaviours, but character traits.

If you spent a week lazing on the sofa watching TV and playing video games, you might think, 'I am a lazy person. I have a spent a week lazing on the sofa.' If you didn't like that view of yourself, you might then think, 'I have to change and stop being lazy.' That's quite a challenge – it's an open-ended change to your character. It would be more helpful to think, 'I spent a week lazing on the sofa. I don't want to act in a lazy way next week.' A target that relates to a week's activities is much less daunting than a target that seems to require that you rewrite your personality.

Changing your mind?

Several studies have shown that if students are made to write an essay proposing or defending a view that is the opposite of their own, they tend to adjust their views to come more into line with the argument they have made.

> '*We are what we pretend to be, so we should be careful about what we pretend to be.*'
> Kurt Vonnegut, *Mother Night* (introduction)

In 1970, Daryl Bem and his colleague Keith McConnell investigated students' views about having control of their own curriculum. The students then had to write an essay proposing the view opposite to their own.

Afterwards, they asked the students what their views had been at the start of the study. The results did not match their pre-study responses: they had adjusted their views, but claimed that they had always held those views.

For advertisers and others in the business of persuading us, that's good news. They only need to home in on something we haven't really thought about or don't have strong views on, get us to think, say or do something in favour of the view they want us to hold, and we'll believe we were always sympathetic to that view.

Back to boring

Daryl Bem adapted Festinger's boring experiment – when he made people carry out a boring task (see page 178 or 263). Bem's participants listened to a tape recording of a man speaking enthusiastically about the boring task.

One group was told the man had been paid twenty dollars for his testimonial, and the other group was told he had been paid one dollar. The participants, when questioned, thought that the man paid only one dollar enjoyed the task more than did those who had been told he was paid twenty dollars.

This is the same result as Festinger got from his participants – those who had been paid only one dollar later recalled the task as more interesting than those who had been paid twenty dollars. Bem concluded that Festinger's subjects were responding in the same way as his own, but the difference was that they were inferring things from their own behaviour rather than from the behaviour of someone else. The process, he argued, was the same – we look at behaviour and infer things about attitude, whether the subject is another person or ourselves.

And earlier...

Long before Bem's experiment, in the 19th century, William James and Carl Lange independently came up with a theory now known, unimaginatively, as the James–Lange theory. They proposed that every stimulus – something we feel, notice, or experience – has a physiological effect on the body. The physiological effect is processed by the brain and creates an emotion. The physiological response is a reflex. So if you see a bear running towards you, your hands might start to sweat and your heart to race. Then your brain notices that reflex and comes up with fear, and the fear makes you take evasive action. The fear then informs your decision about action.

So – can smiling make you happy?

The difficulty with researching whether just smiling makes people happier is that it's necessary to separate the physical act of smiling from a stimulus that might make people happier. It's no use getting people to smile by telling a joke, complimenting them or giving them

TRICK OR TREAT?

A study carried out in 1979 suggests that if we can see ourselves, we are more likely to act in a way we approve of. Researchers observed from hiding places while children going 'trick-or-treating' visited houses at Halloween. When the occupier of the house left the children alone in the entrance hall, saying they may choose one sweet from a selection, 33 per cent of the children took more than one sweet. But if there was a mirror in the hallway, so that the children could see what they were doing, the number who took more than one sweet dropped to less than 4 per cent. It appears that the children didn't want to be seen doing something dishonest, even by themselves, as then they would have to think of themselves as dishonest.

an ice cream, as all of these might make them happier anyway.

A research team headed by Fritz Strack in 1988 used an ingenious method to get participants smiling. They said they were developing new methods to enable paralyzed people to communicate and needed help working with different ways of holding a pencil using just the muscles of the face.

Some participants had to hold the pencil with their teeth; others had to hold it in their lips. The first method forced their faces into a smile, while the second forced them to adopt an unhappier expression. The participants were then

COULD YOU BE A TERRORIST?

In 2010 Rosanna Guadagno and others investigated the methods used by terrorist organizations to recruit and train new members. One strategy was to use the 'foot in the door' technique (see page 231) to draw them in. Once they were involved, though, new recruits were given increasingly extreme tasks. They then seemed to adjust their perception of their own attitudes, aims and beliefs to match the actions they had carried out. Once they started to think of themselves as committed, they would be willing to do more serious tasks. Those tasks confirmed their view of themselves, and a cycle of increasing commitment and extremism set in.

shown cartoons and asked to rate them for humour. The 'smiling' participants found the cartoons funnier.

Real or fake?

A modified version of the study, carried out in 2002, found fake smiling (without raised cheeks) had less of an effect than 'real' smiling (with raised cheeks), and that smiling had an impact on how people perceived positive stimuli but not on their reception of negative stimuli (upsetting or disgusting images). 'Real' smiling still has the effect of lifting mood even if it is faked – it's using all the necessary muscles to replicate a real smile that matters.

So it seems smiling can, in fact, make you happier. It might be a

THE SCIENTIFIC SMILE

The officially accepted smile is called the Duchenne smile. It involves the zygomatic muscles to raise the sides of the mouth and the orbicularis oculi muscles to narrow the eyes. This type of smile is rated by observers as being most genuine.

simple self-perception issue: I'm smiling so I must be happy. But some physiologists have suggested that as smiling exercises the zygomatic muscles, this changes the blood flow to the brain and might actually produce a real effect on brain chemistry.

DOES IT REALLY TAKE MORE MUSCLES TO FROWN THAN TO SMILE?

It's hard to say exactly how many muscles are used for smiling and frowning, especially as people all smile and frown differently. The simplest recognizable smile uses five pairs of muscles, and the simplest frown uses three muscle pairs. If you are just going for economy of muscle use, frowning is the better bet. But that means smiling is better exercise, so perhaps work it into your exercise regime?

Chapter 26

Is it really 'just a stage'?

Do children's minds develop through stages? Or is their development cumulative and layered?

Your toddler is having tantrums, your eight-year-old is answering you back and your teenager is having a strop because you're 'ruining her life'. Don't worry, it's just a stage – they'll grow out of it, everyone says so. Really?

PSYCHOBABBLE: COGNITIVE DEVELOPMENT

Cognitive development is how we acquire knowledge, or how we learn to know things. It looks at how the growing person, from babyhood to adulthood, acquires the mental skills and structures that enable them to deduce, store and use knowledge.

Two models for growing out of being a baby

We are used to thinking of childhood in stages. In everyday life, the stages are a bit woolly, sometimes very short and specific (the bed-wetting stage, the clingy stage) and sometimes seemingly interminable (the stroppy teenager stage). The model of 'stages' of childhood makes the child into something like a train that passes through one station after another, picking up and putting down passengers. Oh look, Temper Tantrums have got on board – they'll be here for a few stops and then get off.

Another model suggests that there is a gradual development in which new skills and abilities are piled on top of old ones, accreting eventually into an adult way of engaging with the world. Ways of being are not left behind, but more are added.

It's a stage they're going through

The stages model is based on the work of Swiss developmental psychologist Jean Piaget (1896–1980). He divided the learning of young children into four stages according to the types of skill they acquired and the ways they could interpret and interact with the world:

AGES 0–2: sensorimotor stage – babies are only aware of their immediate surroundings and themselves. They are highly egocentric, and have no idea that something still exists when they can no longer see it (known as object permanence). However, studies carried out in 1972 suggest that this theory is inaccurate. If a baby is reaching for an offered object and the lights are turned off, the baby continues to reach for it (as revealed by an infra-red camera).

AGES 2–7: pre-operational stage – children are still centred on the external world and

Babies enjoy peep-o as they are delighted to discover the permanence of objects. The predictable reappearance confirms they are right in their conclusion that the parent still exists when no longer visible.

how it works, but can't make logical deductions (which need 'operational' thought). They tend to focus on one aspect of an object or situation at a time. They have difficulty imagining another person's point of view ('theory of mind'), they don't understand principles such as conservation – that the same number of objects can be differently arranged – or the relationship between groups and subgroups of objects. Again, later research suggests that Piaget underestimated what children can do, partly because his experiments were not well designed.

AGES 7–11: concrete operational stage – children can now understand concepts such as conservation of number and volume, but only with the help of physical (concrete) objects to demonstrate them. Later research, once more, suggests that Piaget did not frame his experiments in ways that were accessible to children and so again underestimated their abilities.

AGES 11+: formal operational stage – young people can deal with concepts in their heads and no longer need physical demonstrations to make them real. They can carry out deductive reasoning, understanding, for instance, that if A>B and B>C, then A>C must be true.

Piaget's tests were again criticized. Some researchers have found them to be too culture-specific. Pulawat navigators in Polynesia can carry out complex operational thought to navigate their canoes, yet fail Piaget's tests of development as they are meaningless to them. There has been disagreement, too, about how commonly the fourth stage is ever properly achieved – some research suggests that only a third of the adult population fully achieve the formal operational stage.

Building blocks of behaviour

Jerome Bruner took a different approach, choosing modes, rather than stages in development. In 1966, he proposed that three modes of representation overlay each other, building up a set of skills that are not superseded but all still used in adulthood. He argued that children build a mental 'scaffolding' that supports their learning, with older knowledge supporting new knowledge.

AGES 0-1: enactive mode – babies use action to interact with the world, building 'muscle memory' (such as learning how to wave and walk – skills that are not forgotten except in cases of brain injury).

AGES 1-6: iconic mode – reality is represented through images and sounds.

AGES 7+: symbolic mode

– information is stored and manipulated using symbols such as language and mathematics.

Bruner discovered that some of the tasks Piaget's children failed were better handled if children first talked them through. So, if instead of pouring water from a tall, thin glass into a short, wide glass he first asked them whether there would be more, less or the same amount of water to drink after he had poured it, children then gave the right answer. Some said 'you are only pouring it' – language helped them to work out what would happen and actually accelerated their development.

Combining all modes (enactive, iconic and symbolic) made it easier for them to understand what was happening. If children used a ball of plasticine to make different shapes while simultaneously explaining what they were doing, children readily understood conservation of volume – even if they had earlier failed Piaget's conservation tests.

Inside out or outside in?

Piaget's model is based on development happening from within the child, in a set sequence. Although it requires interaction with the environment and other

'We become ourselves through others.'
Lev Vygotsky, 1896–1934

people, the child is the key component and instigator. Bruner took a different view, making the environment and other people much more important. Children's learning is enabled by adults and other children.

It is through their interaction with others that children come to impart meaning to their actions and sounds. If a child reaches for something and can't grasp it, the other person passes the object to them. They then learn that reaching for something acts as pointing, as that's how it is interpreted. Pointing then becomes an action with its own meaning – a meaning bestowed by the actions of others. This is an 'outside in' way of learning, with influence from the outside world helping to build the child's cognition.

THINKING THE UNTHINKABLE?

Someone's schemas can be structured so that a useful relationship between them is impossible. For example, someone's schema for 'marriage' and their schema for 'homosexuality' might make the concept of gay marriage incomprehensible to them – they can't see how the two words can go together and mean anything. If they are not willing or able to adjust their schemas so that a fit

is possible, they will have to reject gay marriage. Interestingly, people who do reject ideas like this often use words like 'unthinkable' or 'inconceivable' – and that's exactly what such concepts are to them.

How to build a working brain

To make their brains fit for normal, independent life, children have a lot of work to do. First, they build the schemas that they need in order to structure knowledge (see page 223 [in *What did you come in here for?*]). Then they need to assimilate new knowledge by fitting it into their schemas, and modify their schemas to accommodate information that won't fit into them. Luckily, they don't need to know they are doing it.

In fact, we carry on doing this throughout our lives, some more willingly than others. When you meet someone with very entrenched views who simply rejects as 'nonsense' anything they don't want to think about, you are seeing someone who has given up schema-building. There is no place in their schema-set for internet banking or modern art and they can't begin to think about it. It's not the same as investigating it and saying 'no thank you' – it's having a 'closed mind', one in which the schemas have fossilized. The tendency is marked in older people, but we sometimes encounter even quite young people who seem unwilling or unable to take new ideas on board.

As children grow older, they become capable of 'operations' – higher order mental structures that require logical relationships between schemas. Operations make more complex understanding possible. Again, we can see operational failures in people who are resistant to new ideas.

Blank slate or formatted hard drive?

There is an age-old conception of the baby's mind as a *tabula rasa* – a blank slate waiting for knowledge to be written on to it. But there are many challenges to this view. Instinctive and reflex actions are hardwired into the brain. The infant has an instinct to suckle, and does this within minutes of being born, if given the opportunity.

Some things, it's been suggested, are too difficult for a baby to learn from scratch. There might be innate schemas, ready to be populated with knowledge – so instead of a blank slate, a baby's brain is more like a formatted hard drive with all the structures ready to hold knowledge already in place. Noam Chomsky has made a case for language falling into this category, with the child born ready 'primed' to learn a language. He has pointed to the syntactical similarities between languages that make it possible for a baby to populate its language schema with whichever language is used by the family.

SLOWER BRAINS

The neural connections of children and adults are insulated by a fatty coating called a myelin sheath, which speeds the transmission of nerve signals. A baby's brain lacks these myelin sheaths, which develops as the nervous system matures. So babies do actually think slightly more slowly than adults. Children also have limited short-term memory, or 'mental space'.

FERAL CHILDREN AND MISSED CHANCES

Every so often children are discovered living solely with wild animals, having been kept isolated from human contact in one way or another. These tragic cases provide rich pickings for psychologists who can then track the children's development when exposed to other humans, language, and normal human activities and environments.

Children brought up by wolves or wild dogs often run on all fours, howl and growl, and eat raw meat – they act in the same ways as their canine siblings. Some – if found early enough – can integrate into human society. They can learn a language, start to eat cooked food and walk upright. Others, who have missed human contact for longer, might never acquire language or integrate into human society. There seems to be a cut-off point somewhere between six and thirteen. If a child fails to learn a language before that point, they might never be capable of language-learning.

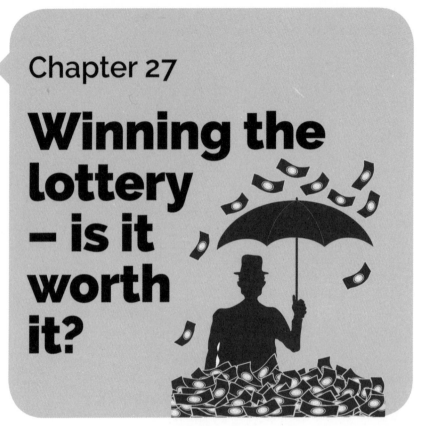

Chapter 27

Winning the lottery – is it worth it?

Do you buy a lottery ticket? Do you want to win?
It might be better if your numbers don't come up.

How often have you dreamed of winning the lottery, or some other stroke of fortune that will make you instantly rich, without the guilt of major fraud or robbery? Many of us have listed the things we'd buy and do if we suddenly had immense wealth. And there are plenty of businesses and national lotteries that feed off those dreams. But would it really make you happy? Or are you wasting your money chasing a dream that will turn sour if realized?

A tax on stupidity?

Why do you buy a lottery ticket, or place a bet at the bookmaker's? Do you really think you might win? Do you hope you might win, even

> '**You aren't buying a chance to win, because there is really no probability that you will win. You are buying the right to fantasize about winning.**'
> Derek Thompson, business editor at *The Atlantic*

though you know you probably won't? Or is it just 'a bit of fun'? What exactly is the fun in handing over money in exchange for a vanishingly small chance of winning so much money it will probably make you miserable?

It's well known that many people who gamble can ill afford it. There's an arrogant assumption among the better off that these people are being stupid – they are wasting money they can't afford on the virtually non-existent chance of winning. But they're not.

They're buying something certain and positive – the opportunity to dream of a better life. Buying the ticket is a passport out of the struggle of everyday life, but it's a tourist visa, not an emigration permit. For the days or hours between buying the ticket and hearing the disappointing result, the ticket-holder is permitted to dream of a better life. It's no more a waste of money than any other transient pleasure, such as a glass of wine or a good meal – and a good deal better for the physical health than many. The point of the ticket is not winning – it's dreaming of winning.

Be careful what you wish for...

Most lottery winners mess up. Studies have found that between 70 per cent and 90 per cent of US lottery winners are broke again within five years – and that's not the worst of it. Apart from poverty, spending on drugs, drink, prostitutes, extravagant consumer goods and dodgy business deals has led many winners to physical and mental ill-health, crime, suicide and even violent death. Several have killed others or themselves in drug- or drink-fuelled accidents.

Most people who are not used to wealth need help dealing with it – otherwise they end up like those overpaid teen stars who go off the rails. The winners who do best in terms of managing their lives post-win are often those who

> ## THE ONLY WAY IS DOWN
> A third of lottery winners end up bankrupt – a study at MIT from 2011 found that winning between $50,000 and $150,000 (£30–90,000) delayed but did not prevent bankruptcy among people in financial difficulty, a finding that suggests cash injections are not the way to help people struggling (how convenient).

use the money for good causes – giving to charity or setting up a trust fund. But why can't we deal with getting what we think we want?

It's all relative

A study carried out in 1978 by Philip Brickman and Dan Coates in the USA studied the happiness level of lottery winners and of paralyzed

> *'The party has ended and it's back to reality. I haven't got two pennies to rub together and that's the way I like it. I find it easier to live off £42 ($70) dole a week than a million.'*
> Michael Carroll, who won £9.7 million ($16 million) in the UK lottery

In 1961, Viv Nicholson won the then-huge sum of £152,319 on the football pools (the equivalent of £2.87 million in 2014). She soon spent her money, and ended up in debt and in trouble with the law. One of her five husbands died when he crashed the car she bought him from her winnings. Her photo is featured on the cover of The Smiths' single 'Heaven Knows I'm Miserable Now'.

accident victims – two sets of people who had experienced significant changes in fortune. They also studied a control group of people who had neither had an accident nor a lottery win. They found that two processes – contrast and habituation – lead to lottery winners being less happy than we might automatically expect.

Peaks and troughs

The point at which a person learns of their lottery win is generally one of ecstatic excitement and pleasure – it is usually a 'peak experience'. It is very difficult for

'I spent 90 per cent of my money on women, drink and fast cars. The rest I wasted.'
George Best, soccer star

later events to match up to the glory of that moment and so the delight people take in smaller pleasures tends to diminish. Lottery winners were found to enjoy mundane pleasures less than people who had not won the lottery.

It doesn't only apply to winning the lottery. Anyone in a career that tends to reach a height and then fade away – especially one that peaks in youth – has to deal with this issue. What does a prime minister do after losing office? Why do ex-sports stars and ex-supermodels sometimes find themselves on a personal downward spiral? Achieving a peak ambition can lead to a sense of emptiness and lack of direction.

Striving for something gives our lives purpose, one that disappears if we achieve our goal. Astrophysicist Dame Jocelyn Bell Burnell, who was controversially excluded from the Nobel Prize for Physics for her discovery of pulsars (the Nobel prize committee gave the credit for that to her thesis supervisor,

Jocelyn Bell Burnell makes the most of not having won a Nobel prize for her discovery of pulsars.

Antony Hewish) has said she is glad she didn't win, as where would there be left to go after that? She wouldn't be able to take as much pleasure in other prizes as they'd never match up to the Nobel. She has since been showered with honours, including her damehood.

Winner's (bad) luck

The moment of winning is a poisoned chalice because it diminishes future successes. But even the pleasures we imagine we would enjoy if we were rich diminish over time as we become accustomed to them. Habituation makes them less special.

People quickly become used to their home always being warm, to always having the best food and going to the best hotels and restaurants. Apparently, people can even become used to and jaded by being driven by a chauffeur in a flashy car and sipping cocktails on palm-fringed beaches. The exotic becomes mundane – when everything is special, nothing is special.

At the same time, it becomes harder to take pleasure in small events such as receiving a compliment or watching a favourite

LUCKY NUMBERS?

Some people always buy the same lottery numbers, often choosing ones that have some personal significance, such as a string of birthdates or a number they consider 'lucky'. The more times their numbers don't come up, the better they think their chances are of winning in the near future. Even if they know the maths, they engage in some kind of mystical thinking that encourages them to believe that every number must have its turn. In fact, there is no greater likelihood that a random sequence of numbers will appear than that a sequence like 1, 2, 3, 4, 5 and 6 will come up.

The website for the UK lottery publishes a list of the numbers that win most and least, and of those most 'overdue' – those that haven't come up for a while. But every draw is random, of course, and the results of previous draws have no impact on future results. It could be that the same six numbers appear every week for a year – it's just not very likely.

But if you *do* want to play the lottery, and do want to risk winning lots of money, don't pick the same numbers that everyone else chooses. This means avoid following an obvious pattern. Of course, if you want to win only a modest amount to limit the damage the win does to your life, picking – say – the first six prime numbers should guarantee that if your numbers do come up you will have to share them with lots of other people.

television programme. The lottery winners reported less enjoyment of these things than either the control group or the accident victims. Nor did they expect to be happier in the future. Over the long term, the winners had no gain in happiness over the control group. When Brickman and Coates questioned victims of serious accidents, whose fortunes had therefore taken a major downturn, the researchers discovered that they, too, contrasted their previous life with their current situations. The comparison made them more miserable, especially as they tended to view their past situation through rose-tinted spectacles, remembering it as more pleasurable than it really seemed at the time. This heightened their sense of loss.

DO PIGEONS DREAM OF WINNING THE LOTTERY?

You might think that gambling is a particularly human behaviour. Not so. Given two options, one of which produces food 50 per cent of the time and the other produces food 75 per cent of the time, pigeons strongly prefer the first option. It seems that the thrill of the gamble appeals to the pigeons. So perhaps the kick humans get out of gambling is, at some basal level, biological. When you buy a lottery ticket, you are being no smarter than a pigeon...

The last page

Who is this?
What happened?
Did you remember?
She featured on page 222
[*What did you come in here
for?*]

What does
***anagnorisis* mean?**
Are you corpulent?
If you didn't
remember what
anagnorisis means,
this clue might help
– are you married to
your mother? (Page
223)

PICTURE CREDITS

Anne Rooney: 195. Ansgar Walk: 11. Bridgeman: 185 (Private Collection/Look and Learn). Bundesarchiv, Bild: 57. Carl Lender: 42. Clipart: 15, 31, 39, 40, 51, 105, 113, 153. Corbis: 37 (Ann Kaplan), 70 (Hulton-Deutsch Collection), 97, 103 (Bettmann), 181 (Sunset Boulevard), 187 (CinemaPhoto), 204 (Matthew Aslett/Demotix), 221 (CHIP EAST/Reuters). Foto Ad Meskens: 8. Gaetan Lee: 28. Getty: 84 (Time & Life Pictures), 131, 154 (NY Daily News), 173 (Fox Photos), 242 (NY Daily News), 298. Kobal Collection: 54, 100. Lorna Tilley: 60. Mary Parrish: 118t. NASA: 196tr, 196tl. National Photo Company Collection: 75. nyenyec: 49. OpenStax College: 20. Peter Trevaris: 16. Science and Society Picture Library: 299 (Daily Herald Archive/National Media Museum). Shutterstock: 7, 9, 10, 19, 24, 25, 27 (Monkey Business Images), 29, 33, 34, 36, 38, 46, 52, 58, 62, 63, 64, 66 (spirit of america), 67 (Joe Speer), 71t, 73, 77 (Antoine Begeler), 80, 87, 88, 91, 92, 94, 109, 114, 115, 116, 118b, 120, 123, 124, 125, 130, 133, 144, 149, 150 (Canada panda), 152t (PiXXart), 152b, 158, 160, 167, 170, 175, 177, 179, 180, 189, 192b, 203, 207, 209, 212 (Barone Firenze), 214, 215, 217, 218, 219, 223, 226, 227t, 227b, 229, 230, 233 (skyfish), 241, 243 (bibiphoto), 247, 254, 256, 257, 258, 261, 262 (Rob Wilson), 267, 270, 272, 273, 278, 279, 282 (Oleg Golovnov), 283, 285, 287, 289, 290, 293, 294, 296t, 296b, 300, 302. W. E. F. Britten/Adam Cuerden: 129. Wellcome Library, London: 6, 13, 47, 83.